To Anne

The Best of the Best!

Love,

Elaine

12/02

knits

for

Barbie®

doll

knits for Barbie doll

75 fabulous fashions for knitting

by

Nicky Epstein

SOHO PUBLISHING COMPANY
NEW YORK

SOHO PUBLISHING COMPANY
233 Spring Street
New York, New York 10013

EDITOR-IN-CHIEF
Trisha Malcolm

ART DIRECTOR
Chi Ling Moy

BOOK MANAGER
Theresa McKeon

CONTRIBUTING EDITORS
Betty Christiansen
Annemarie McNamara

INSTRUCTIONS EDITORS
Carla Scott
Karen Greenwald
Charlotte Parry

YARN EDITOR
Veronica Manno

INSTRUCTIONS PROOFREADER
Nancy Henderson

PHOTOGRAPHY
Bobb Connors

STYLISTS
Christina Batch
Lisa Ventry

PRODUCTION MANAGERS
Lillian Esposito
David Joinnides

PRESIDENT, SOHO PUBLISHING COMPANY
Art Joinnides

Library of Congress Cataloging-in-Publication Data

Knits for Barbie Doll / by Nicky Epstein.
      p. cm.
    ISBN 1-931543-05-4
    1. Doll clothes–Patterns. 2. Knitting–Patterns. 3. Barbie dolls–Clothing. I. Epstein, Nicky.

  TT175.7 .K67 2001
  746.43'2041–dc21   2001020626

Manufactured in China

1 3 5 7 9 10 8 6 4 2

First Edition

In 1959, my parents bought me the original Barbie® Doll, and it was such a happy day in my life! With the help of my mother and grandmother, I began knitting and crocheting clothes for my new doll. It is now, years later, a privilege for me to be the author of the first book featuring a collection of knit designs for Barbie—and happily, the mere mention of working on this book has put a smile on the face of everyone I've told!

For me, the greatest challenge was designing for one of the world's most famous ladies. With that in mind, this collection of knits was designed for "real girls", with style, whimsy and originality as my guidelines. Included are knits for Ken®, as well as for two of Barbie dolls four-legged friends, and cozy afghans, pillows and a rug for her home. The designs are knitter-friendly, and easy enough for knitters of all ages and experience.

Be warned—knitting for Barbie can be addictive! If you find yourself with an abundance of lovely little hand-knit clothes, you may want to donate them to hospitals or church bazaars, give them as gifts, hang them on your Christmas tree, away from lights or open flames, or frame them as works of art. You may just want to give them to those who will cherish the fact that they were lovingly made by you.

Knitting the garments for this book was so much fun, I hope knitting for Barbie gives you as much pleasure as it has given me. Most of all, I hope Barbie and her fans will be pleased with her new "handknit" wardrobe.

Happy Knitting for your Barbie® Doll,

To my parents, Carmella and Benjamin Quinones who bought me my first Barbie® Doll.

Table of Contents

Classic Cable Pullover

A twist on the original. As classic as the lady who wears it, this Aran pullover wraps Barbie in a rich Irish tradition. Knit with ecru wool, in keeping with the fishermen's sweaters of old, this tunic-length sweater features a baby cable stitch pattern across the center front. Ribbed borders and stockinette-stitch sleeves and background frame and enhance the cabled front.

Yarn
Paternayan Persian by JCA
(approx 8yd/7.4m) wool
5 skeins in #263 cream
Needles
Size 2 (2.5mm) needles or
size needed to obtain gauge
Accessories
1 small snap

CABLE PATTERN
3RT
K the 3rd st on the LH needle,
then k the 2nd st and then k the
first st, drop all 3 sts from LH needle
at once.
Row 1 K4, *p2, k3; rep from *, end
p2, k4.
Rows 2 and 4 P4, *k2, p3; rep
from *, end k2, p4.
Row 3 K4, *p2, 3RT; rep from *, end
p2, k4.
Rep rows 1-4 for cable pat.

sweater

BACK
Cast on 20 sts. Work in k1, p1 rib for
2 rows. Work in St st until piece
measures 4½" from beg. Bind off.

FRONT
Cast on 20 sts. Work in k1, p1 rib for
2 rows.
Next row (RS) Knit, inc 5 sts evenly
spaced across row—25 sts. P 1 row.
Work in cable pat until piece
measures 4" from beg, end with
WS row.

Neck Shaping
Work 6 sts, join new yarn, bind off
center 13 sts, work to end. Working
both sides at once, dec 1 st each
neck edge on next RS row—5 sts.
Work even until front measures
same length as back. Bind off 5 sts
each side for shoulders.

SLEEVES
Cast on 10 sts. Work in k1, p1 rib for
2 rows. Work in St st, inc 1 st each
side on next row, then every 4th
row 3 times—18 sts. Work even
until sleeve measures 3" from beg.
Bind off.
Neckband
Cast on 28 sts. Work in k1, p1 rib for
4 rows. Bind off in rib. Sew
neckband seam.

FINISHING
Block pieces. Sew shoulder seams.
Sew neckband to neck edge,
centering seam at center back. Place
markers 1½" down from shoulders
on front and back. Sew sleeves
between markers. Sew side and
sleeve seams.

note

Use 2 plys of yarn held tog
throughout.

gauge

6 sts and 9 rows to 1" over
St st using size 2 (2.5mm)
needles and 2 plys of yarn
held tog.
FOR PROPER FIT, TAKE THE
TIME TO CHECK YOUR GAUGE.

Sweetheart Pullover

Hearts a–flutter. America's sweetheart is irresistible in this coy, cropped pullover, worked in three shades of her signature pink. The rosy sweater body is worked in basic stockinette with the heart motif stitched afterward in duplicate stitch. Fuchsia warms the heart and dots the dainty ribbed edges—worked in palest pink—with touches of color.

Yarn
Paternayan Persian by JCA
(approx 8yd/7.4m) wool
4 skeins of #945 pink (A),
1 skein each of #942 bright
pink (B) and #947 light
pink (C).
Needles
Size 3 (3mm) needles or size
to obtain gauge
Accessories
1 small snap

pullover

BACK
With C cast on 21 sts. Work in k1,
p1 rib for 2 rows.
Next row (RS) Change to A and
work in St st for 1¾".
Next row (RS) K10, join new yarn
and bind off 1 st, work to end. Work
both sides at once for 1¼". Bind off.

FRONT
Work same as for back, omitting
opening, until piece measures 3"
from beg.
Neck Shaping
K6, join new yarn, bind off center 5
sts, k6. Dec 1 st at each neck edge
every other row once—5 sts each
side. Work even until front measures
same as back. Bind off.

SLEEVES
With C cast on 12 sts. Work in k1,
p1 rib for 2 rows.
Next row (RS) Change to A and
work in St st, inc 1 st each side
every 4th row 3 times—18 sts. Work
even until piece measures 3" from
beg. Bind off.

FINISHING
Sew shoulder seams
Neckband
With C, pick up and k 22 sts evenly
around neck edge. Work in k1, p1 rib
for 2 rows. Bind off.
Heart
With B, duplicate st heart foll chart,
centering heart on front.
Embroidery
With B and using a running st,
embroider the rib bands of the lower
edge, sleeves and collar.
Place markers 1½"down from
shoulders on front and back. Sew
sleeves between markers. Sew
side and sleeve seams. Sew snap
at neckband.

Color Key

☐ Pink A

⬤ Red B

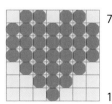

7 sts

note

Use 2 plys of yarn held tog
throughout.

gauge

6 sts and 9 rows to 1" over St
st using size 3 (3mm) needles
and 2 plys of yarn held tog.
FOR PROPER FIT, TAKE THE
TIME TO CHECK YOUR GAUGE.

Cozy Christmas Pullover

Who wouldn't love to find this candlelight-colored treat under her tree? The hip length and rolled collar, cuffs, and hem are pulled straight from today's fashion pages, and the Christmas tree motif, worked in intarsia and trimmed with tiny glass beads, makes it a casual but classy holiday must-have. A perfect primer for intarsia if you're new to the technique.

Yarn
Paternayan Persian by JCA
(approx 8yd/7.4m) wool
5 skeins in #710 Mustard (A)
1 skein in #611 Loden (B)
Small amount of gold
metallic thread
Needles
Size 2 (2.5mm) needles or
size needed to obtain gauge
Accessories
Small multi-colored beads
1 snap

pullover

BACK
With A, cast on 20 sts. Work in St st
for 2¾".
Armhole Shaping
Bind off 2 sts at beg of next 2
rows—16 sts. Work 2 rows even.
Neck Opening
Next row (RS) K8, join new yarn,
k8. Working each side at once, cont
in St st until back opening measures
1". Bind off.

FRONT
Work as for back until piece
measures 1½" from beg.
Beg Chart
K5 A, work 10 sts of chart, work to
end. Work through row 12 of chart,
working armhole shaping as for back
when piece measures 2¾". Then cont
in St st with A for 6 rows.
Neck Shaping
Next row (RS) K6, join new yarn
and bind off center 4 sts, k6.
P 1 row.
Next row Dec 1 st each neck edge—
5 sts. When piece measures same as
back to shoulder, bind off.

SLEEVES
With A, cast on 12 sts. Work in
St st, inc 1 st each side every 4th
row 3 times—18 sts. Work even
until piece measures 3¾" from beg.
Bind off.

FINISHING
Sew shoulder seams.
Neckband
With A, pick up and k 20 sts around
neck. Work in St st for 1". Bind off.
Set in sleeves. Sew side and sleeve
seams. Sew snap to back neck.
Sew beads on tree for ornaments.
With metallic thread, sew star to
top of tree.
Neck, sleeve and lower edges will
roll naturally.

note

Use 2 plys of yarn held tog
throughout.

Color Key

▢ Mustard A

⬤ Loden B

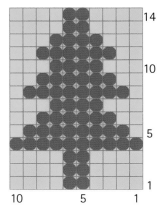

gauge

6 sts and 9 rows to 1" over St
st using size 2 (2.5mm)
needles and 2 plys of yarn
held tog.
FOR PROPER FIT, TAKE THE
TIME TO CHECK YOUR GAUGE.

Chic Textured Pullover

Weekend getaway. Whether she's heading out to the country or into the heart of the Big City, this seed-stitch, ruby red pullover is sure to be in the overnight bag of every classy lady. Ribbed edges finish the knit one, purl one stitch pattern, and the simple dropped sleeves require no shaping.

seed stitch

Row 1 *K1, p1; rep from * across.
Row 2 K the purl sts and p the knit sts.
Rep row 2 for seed st.

pullover

BACK

Cast on 20 sts. Work in k1, p1 rib for 2 rows, dec 1 st each side of last row—18 sts. Work even in seed st until piece measures 4" from beg. Bind off.

FRONT

Work as for back until piece measures 3½", end with a WS row.
Neck Shaping
Work 6 sts, join new yarn and bind off center 6 sts, work to end. Working both sides at once, dec 1 st each neck edge—5 sts each side. Work even until piece measures same length as back. Bind off 5 sts each side.

SLEEVES

Cast on 12 sts. Work in k1, p1 rib for 2 rows. Work in seed st for 4 rows.
Next row Inc I st each side once, then every 4th row twice—18 sts. Work even until sleeve measures 3" from beg. Bind off.

FINISHING

Sew shoulder seams.
Neckband
Cast on 28 sts. Work in k1, p1 rib for 4 rows. Bind off in rib. Sew neckband tog. Sew neckband to neck edge centering neckband seam at center back neck edge.
Place markers 1¾" down from shoulders on front and back. Sew sleeves between markers. Sew side and sleeve seams.

materials

Yarn
Paternayan Persian by JCA (approx 8yd/7.4m) wool
5 skeins in # 968 red
Needles
Size 2 (2.5mm) needles or size needed to obtain gauge

note

Use 2 plys of yarn held tog throughout.

gauge

5 sts and 11 rows to 1" over seed st using size 2 (2.5mm) needles and 2 plys of yarn held tog.
FOR PROPER FIT, TAKE THE TIME TO CHECK YOUR GAUGE.

Cashmere Turtleneck and Cardigan

Shades of grey. Barbie® and Ken® are the picture of casual elegance in these coordinating sweaters. Ken's smart cardigan features raglan sleeves, a shawl collar, and a buttoned front.

CARDIGAN
Yarn
Cashmere by Grignasco/JCA
.88oz/25g (approx
120yd/110m) cashmere
1 ball in #581 gray
Needles
Sizes 1 and 2 (2.25 and
2.5mm) needles or size
needed to obtain gauge
Accessories
Stitch holders

cardigan for Ken®

BACK
With smaller needles, cast on 28 sts.
Work in k1, p1 rib for 3 rows.
Next row (WS) Change to larger
needles and work in St st until piece
measures 2½" from beg.
Raglan Shaping
Bind off 2 sts at beg of next 2 rows.
Next row (RS) K1, ssk, k to last 3
sts, k2tog, k1. P 1 row.
Rep last 2 rows 6 times more—10
sts. Place sts on holder.

LEFT FRONT
With smaller needles, cast on 13 sts.
Work as for back until piece
measures 2½" from beg.
Raglan and Neck Shaping
Next row (RS) Bind off 2 sts, work
to end. P 1 row.
Next row K1, ssk, k to last 3 sts,
k2tog, k1. P 1 row. Cont raglan
shaping as for back at beg of RS
rows, AND AT THE SAME TIME, dec 1
st at neck edge every 6th row once—
2 sts. Place sts on holder.

RIGHT FRONT
Work to correspond to left front,
reversing all shaping.

SLEEVES
With smaller needles cast on 16 sts.
Work in k1, p1 rib for 3 rows.
Next row (WS) Change to larger
needles and work in St st, inc 1 st
each side every 6th row 3 times—22
sts. Work even until piece measures
2¾" from beg.
Raglan Shaping
Bind off 2 sts at beg of next 2 rows.
Next (dec) row (RS) K1, ssk, k to
last 3 sts, k2tog, k1. P 1 row. Rep
last 2 rows 6 times more—4 sts.
Place sts on a holder.

POCKETS
With smaller needles, cast on 7 sts.
Work in k1, p1 rib for 2 rows.
Bind off.

gauge

8 sts and 10 rows to 1" over
St st using 2 (2.5mm) larger
needles and Cashmere yarn.
FOR PROPER FIT, TAKE THE
TIME TO CHECK YOUR GAUGE.

Barbie® is ever the image of cool sophistication in her cropped, raglan-sleeved turtleneck. Both tops can be stitched from one ball of soft grey cashmere.

FINISHING

Sew raglan sleeves into raglan armhole.

Front Bands and Collar

With RS facing and smaller needles, pick up and k 23 sts (including sts from holders) along right front edge to first neck dec, pm, pick up 41 sts around back neck to first neck dec of left front, pm, 23 sts along left front edge—87 sts. Work 3 rows in k1, p1 rib.

Beg Short Row Shaping

Next row (RS) Rib to 2nd marker, turn.

Next row (WS) Rib to marker, turn.

Next row (RS) Rib to last 4 sts before marker, turn.

Next row Rib to last 4 sts before marker, turn. Cont as established, working 4 sts less each time 6 times more, turn and rib to end. Bind off in rib.

Sew side and sleeve seams. Sew on buttons evenly spaced along left band. Sew pockets to fronts.

turtleneck for Barbie®

BACK

With smaller needles, cast on 35 sts. Work in k1, p1 rib for ½", end with a WS row. Change to larger needles and work in St st until piece measures 1¾" from beg.

Divide for Front and Back

Next row (RS) K8 (left back), bind off next 2 sts, k until 15 sts from bind-off (front), bind off next 2 sts, k to end (right back).

RIGHT BACK

P8, sl rem sts to holder. Work even in St st for 2 rows.

Raglan Shaping

Next row (RS) K1, k2tog, k to end. P 1 row.

Rep last 2 rows 3 times more—4 sts. Place sts on a holder.

FRONT

Purl next 15 sts from holder, leave rem 8 sts on holder. Work in St st for 2 rows.

Raglan Shaping

Next row (RS) K1, k2tog, k to last 3 sts, k2tog, k1. P 1 row. Rep last 2 rows 3 times more—7 sts. Place sts on a holder.

LEFT BACK
Purl across rem 8 sts from first holder. Work in St st for 2 rows.
Raglan Shaping
Next row (RS) K to last 3 sts, k2tog, k1. P 1 row. Rep last 2 rows 3 times more—4 sts. Place sts on a holder.

SLEEVES
With smaller needles, cast on 12 sts. Work in k1, p1 rib for ¾". Change to larger needles and work in St st, inc 1 st each side every 4th row 4 times—20 sts. Work even until piece measures 2¾" from beg, end with a WS row.

Raglan Shaping
Bind off 2 sts at beg of next 2 rows—16 sts. P 1 row.
Next (dec) row (RS) K1, k2tog, k to last 3 sts, k2tog, k1. P 1 row. Rep last 2 rows 5 times more—4 sts. Place sts on a holder.

FINISHING
Block pieces. Sew raglan sleeves into raglan armhole. Sew sleeve seams.
Turtleneck
With RS facing and smaller needles, work across sts from holders. Inc 4 sts evenly across—27 sts.
Work in k1, p1 rib for 1". Bind off in rib. Sew back seam including turtleneck.

materials

TURTLENECK
Yarn
Cashmere by Grignasco/JCA .88oz/25g (approx 120yd/110m) cashmere 1 ball in #581 gray
Needles
Sizes 1 and 2 (2.25 and 2.5mm) needles or size needed to obtain gauge
Accessories
Stitch holders and markers
5 JHB buttons #474370

note

TURTLENECK
Front and back of turtleneck are made in one piece to the armhole.

gauge

8 sts and 10 rows to 1" over St st using 2 (2.5mm) needles and Cashmere yarn.
FOR PROPER FIT, TAKE THE TIME TO CHECK YOUR GAUGE.

Retro Poncho

Good vibrations. This hip '60s-style poncho is made by knitting two triangles with a simple stripe pattern, then sewing them together to make the colorful V-shaping and cool corners in the front and back. A garter-stitch neckline and funky fringe finish the look. The tapestry wool it's knit in comes in doll-sized skeins and a rainbow of retro colors.

stripe pattern

Work in St st as foll;
7 rows A
2 rows E
3 rows C
Next row *K1 B, k1 C; rep from *
to end.
1 row B
4 rows D
Next row K1 B, k1 D; rep from *
to end.
1 row B
2 rows E
10 rows A

poncho

(make 2)
With A, cast on 48 sts. Work 2 rows
in St st. Beg in stripe pat.
Next (dec) row K1, k2tog, k to last
3 sts, ssk, k1—46 sts. Cont in stripe
pat and rep dec row every other row
14 times more—18 sts.
Shoulder Shaping
Next row (RS) With A, k1, k2tog,
k4, k2tog, ssk, k4, ssk, k1—14 sts.
P 1 row.
Next row (RS) K1, k2tog, k2, k2tog,
ssk, k2, ssk, k1—10 sts.
K 3 rows. Bind off

FINISHING
Sew back seam. Sew front seam
leaving 1" open for neck.
Fringe
Cut 2" lengths of A. Attach fringe
using crochet hook.

materials

Yarn
Paternayan Persian by JCA
(approx 8yd/7.4m) wool
3 skeins in #702 gold (A)
1 skein each in #501 blue (B),
#670 green (C), #811 orange
(D) and #940 red (E)
Needles
Size 2 (2.5mm) needles or
size needed to obtain gauge
Size C/2 (2.5mm) crochet
hook

note

Use 2 plys of yarn held tog
throughout.

gauge

13 sts and 18 rows to 2" over
St st using size 2 (2.5mm)
needles and 2 plys of yarn
held tog.
FOR PROPER FIT, TAKE THE
TIME TO CHECK YOUR GAUGE.

Tennis Cardigan

Game-set-match! This versatile cardigan isn't just for the courts—Barbie® serves up style no matter where she sports it. Knit in an easy mock cable pattern, its texture of diminutive twists is deceptively simple to create—no tiny cable needle is necessary. Ribbed trim pulls it all together, on the cuffs and hem as well as around the neckline.

Yarn
Richesse Et Soie by Knit One,
Crochet Two, .88oz/25g
(approx 145yd/132m)
cashmere/silk
1 ball in #9243 sunrise

Needles
Size 1 (2.25mm) needles or
size needed to obtain gauge
Tapestry needle

Accessories
4 JHB white doll buttons,
#13055
4 small snaps for closure
(optional)

CABLE PATTERN
Rows 1 and 3 (WS) K2, *p2, k2; rep
from * to end.
Row 2 P2, *k2, p2; rep from *
to end.
Row 4 P2, *knit the second st on LH
needle, then knit the first st and sl
both sts from needle tog, p2; rep
from * to end.
Rep rows 1-4 for cable pat.

cardigan

BACK
Cast on 26 sts. Work in k1, p1 rib for
3 rows. Work in cable pat until piece
measures 3½" from beg. Bind off.

LEFT FRONT
Cast on 14 sts. Work as for back
until piece measures 2" from beg,
end with a RS row.
Neck Shaping
Next row (WS) Bind off at neck
edge 1 st every other row 5 times—9
sts. Work even until same length as
back. Bind off.

RIGHT FRONT
Work to correspond to left front,
reversing all shaping.

SLEEVES
Cast on 14 sts. Work in k1, p1 rib for
3 rows. Work cable pat, inc 1 st
each side every 4th row 3 times—20
sts. Work even until piece measures
3" from beg. Bind off.

FINISHING
Sew shoulder seams.
Front and Neck Bands
With RS facing, beg at lower right
front, pick up and k 34 sts to neck,
11 sts across back and 34 sts from
left front—79 sts. Work in k1, p1 rib
for 4 rows. Bind off.
Place markers 1½" down from
shoulders on front and back. Sew
sleeves between markers. Sew side
and sleeve seams.
Sew 4 buttons to left front.
Optional: Sew snaps to fronts
under buttons.

gauge

9 sts and 12 rows to 1" over
cable pat using size 1
(2.25mm) needles and
Richesse Et Soie.
FOR PROPER FIT, TAKE THE
TIME TO CHECK YOUR GAUGE.

Summertime Sailor Sets

Anchors away. These outfits are just the thing for a weekend of sailing. Inspired by traditional sailor suits, the sailor top and pant set is made of cotton in red, white, and blue. The small-scale striped top with red trim and tie is worked in stockinette stitch, as are the navy pants, trimmed with doll-sized buttons.

sailor pants

(make 2)
With A, beg at waist and cast on 20 sts. Work in k1, p1 rib for 2 rows. Then work in St st for 1½".

Crotch Shaping
Cast on 2 sts at beg of next 2 rows—24 sts. Work even for 1½".

Leg Shaping
Dec 1 st at beg of next 2 rows, then every 6th row 3 times more—16 sts. Work even until piece measures 6¾" from beg. Bind off.

FINISHING
With sewing thread, sew front, back, and leg seams. Weave elastic thread through ribbing at waist and pull to gather. Sew a vertical row of 3 red buttons along each side of front seam.

sailor top

With B, cast on 41 sts. Work in St st and stripes pat of 2 rows B, 1 row C, and when piece measures 1¼" from beg, end with a WS row

Armhole Shaping
Next row (RS) K9 (left back) and sl to holder, bind off 2 sts, k19 (front) and sl to holder, bind off 2 sts, k9 (right back).

RIGHT BACK

Next row (WS) Work even in St st and stripe pat until armhole measures 1¾". Bind off.

FRONT
Join yarn and p across next 19 sts from st holder.

V-Neck Shaping
P9, join new yarn and bind off center st, p9. Working both sides at once, in St st and stripe pat, dec 1 st at each neck edge on next row, then every 3rd row twice more—6 sts, each side. Work even until armhole measures same as right back. Bind off 6 sts each side.

LEFT BACK
Join yarn and p9 sts from holder. Work even in St st and stripe pat until armhole measures 1¾". Bind off.

MIDDY COLLAR
With B, cast on 21 sts. Work 2 rows in St st. Change to C and k 1 row. Change to B and work even in St st until piece measures 1" from beg, end with a WS row.

Neck Shaping
Next row (RS) K7, join new yarn and bind off 7 sts, k7. Working both sides at once, dec 1 st at each neck edge on next row, then every 3rd row 3 times—3 sts each side.
Next row (RS) K1, [k2tog] twice,

SAILOR SET
Yarn
Knit-Cro Sheen by J & P Coats (approx 100yds/92m) cotton 1 ball each in #182 true blue (A), #001 white (B) and #126 red (C)

Needles
Size 2 (2.5mm) needles or size needed to obtain gauge
Size B/1 (2mm) crochet hook
Sewing needle

Accessories
Stitch holders
Matching sewing thread
Elastic thread
6 Barbie buttons from JHB in Red
Small metal snaps

notes

SAILOR SET
Use 2 strands of yarn held tog throughout for knitting and for crochet edging.

SAILOR TOP
Back and front are worked in one piece to the underarm.

gauge

15 sts and 19 rows to 2" over St st using size 2 (2.5mm) needles and 2 strands of yarn held tog.
FOR PROPER FIT, TAKE THE TIME TO CHECK YOUR GAUGE.

Sailor Short Set

The red playsuit is perfect for splashing in the sea, tipped with navy trim and tiny white buttons. A white rolled-brim hat protects Barbie® doll's fair complexion from too much sun.

k1—4 sts, thus joining sides. P 1 row.
Next row (RS) SK2P, k1. Bind off rem 2 sts.

Ties and Edging
With crochet hook and C, ch 12 (for tie). With RS of collar facing, join chain with a slip st at top right edge above center point and ch 1. Work row of sc evenly around entire outer edge, working 2 sc in each corner. Ch 12 (for tie) and fasten off. Knot ties.

FINISHING
With matching sewing thread, sew shoulder seams.
Edging
With RS facing and B, work a row of sc evenly along each side of back opening.
Sew two snaps to back opening. With matching sewing thread, sew middy collar to front at V-neck shaping.

white sailor hat

With B, cast on 43 sts. P 1 row, k 1 row.
Next (dec) row (RS) *K3, k2tog: rep from *, end k3—35 sts.
K 1 row, p 1 row, then work in St st for 6 rows.
Next (dec) row K1 *SK2P; rep from *, end k1—13 sts.
Next row P2tog across, p1—7 sts.
Next row K2tog across, k1-4 sts, pass last 3 sts over 1st on needle and fasten off.
Sew back seam.

red shorts

(make 2)
With A, beg at waist and cast on 20 sts. Work in k1, p1 rib for 2 rows. Then work in St st for 1½".
Crotch Shaping
Cast on 2 sts at beg of next 2 rows—24 sts. Work even until piece measures 3" from beg. Bind off.

FINISHING
With sewing thread, sew front, back, and leg seams. Weave elastic thread through ribbing at waist and pull to gather.

RED PLAYSUIT
Yarn
Knit-Cro Sheen by J & P Coats
(approx 150yds/135m) cotton
1 ball in #126 red (A)
Small amounts in #182 true
blue (B)
Needles
Size 2 (2.5mm) needles or
size needed to obtain gauge
Size B/1 (2mm) crochet hook
Sewing needle
Accessories
Stitch holders
Matching sewing thread
Elastic thread
3 Barbie buttons from JHB in
white
Small metal snaps

red top

With B, cast on 41 sts. Work in St st
for 2 rows. Change to A and cont in
St until piece measures 1¾" from
beg, end with a WS row.
Armhole Shaping
Next row (RS) K9 (left back) and sl
to holder, bind off 2 sts, k19 (front)
and sl to holder, bind off 2 sts, k9
(right back).

RIGHT BACK
Next row (WS) Work even in
St st until armhole measures 1¾".
Bind off.

FRONT
Join yarn and p across next 19 sts
from holder.
V-Neck Shaping
P9, join new yarn and bind off
center st, p9. Working both sides
once, dec 1 st at each neck edge on
next row, then every 3rd row twice
more—6 sts. Work even until
armhole measures same as right
back. Bind off 6 sts each side.

LEFT BACK
Join yarn and p9 sts from holder.
Work even in St st until armhole
measures 1¾". Bind off.

FINISHING
With matching sewing thread, sew
shoulder seams.
Edging
With RS facing, crochet hook and B,
work a row of sc evenly around
armholes and along each side of
back opening.
Sew two snaps to back opening.
Sew a vertical row of 3 white
buttons to center front.

note

Red top: Back and front are
worked in one piece to the
underarm.

gauge

15 sts and 19 rows to 2" over
St st using size 2 (2.5mm)
needles and 2 strands of yarn
held tog.
FOR PROPER FIT, TAKE THE
TIME TO CHECK YOUR GAUGE.

Cozy Cable Afghan and Pillow
Plush "Fur" Rug

Think pink.
The lush rug is made extra special with a novelty fur yarn that needs only a garter stitch to create a carpet confection. The soft, striped afghan features a baby mock cable pattern and is knit in five separate color stripes, then sewn together. The pillow matches the afghan perfectly with sweet pink cables and tufts of fluff at each corner.

rug

(rug is reversible)
With A, cast on 53 sts.
Rows 1–6 Knit.
Row 7 With A k4, *with B k1, with A k3; rep from *, end k4 A.
Row 8 With A only k4, *p1, k3; rep from *, end k4.
Rep these 8 rows 8 times more.
K 6 rows A. Bind off.

CABLE PATTERN

Rows 1 and 3 (WS) K2, *p2, k2; rep from * to end.
Row 2 (RS) P2, *k2, p2; rep from * to end.
Row 4 P2, *k2tog but leave sts on needle, knit the first st again, sl both sts off needle tog, p2; rep from * to end.
Rep rows 1-4 for cable pat.

afghan

(make 3 strips in A and 2 strips in B)
Cast on 14 sts. Work in cable pat, working 4-row rep 16 times, then work rows 1-3. Bind off.

FINISHING

Sew strips tog as foll: A, B, A, B, A.
Fringe
Cut 2" lengths of A. With 2 strands held tog, use crochet hook to attach fringe to top and bottom. Trim evenly.

pillow

With A, cast on 22 sts. Work in cable pat, working 4-row rep 5 times. Bind off

FINISHING

Fold in half, with WS tog, sew sides. Stuff with fiberfill. Sew last side closed.
Fringe
Cut eight 2" lengths of A. With 2 strands held tog, use crochet hook to attach fringe to each corner. Trim evenly.

RUG
Yarn
Furore by Lang/Berroco, Inc. 1³/₄oz/50g (approx 94yd/86m) nylon
1 skein each of #7009 pink (A) and #7020 blue (B)
Small amount fiberfill for pillow stuffing
Needles
Size 3 (3mm) needles or size needed to obtain gauge
AFGHAN AND PILLOW
Yarn
Jamie 3 Ply by Lion Brand Yarn Co., 1³/₄oz/50g (approx 196yds/180m) acrylic
1 skein each in #201 pink (A) and #200 white (B)
Needles
Size 3 (3mm) needles or size needed to obtain gauge
Small crochet hook
Accessories
Fiberfill for pillow stuffing

sizes
RUG
10" x 8"
AFGHAN
7" x 9" (including fringe)
PILLOW
3" x 2¹/₂" (stuffed)

gauges
RUG
10¹/₂ sts and 19¹/₂ rows to 2" over pat st using size 3 (3mm) needles and Furore.
AFGHAN AND PILLOW
10 sts and 9 rows to 1" over cable pat using size 3 (3mm) needles and Jamie Baby.
FOR PROPER FIT, TAKE THE TIME TO CHECK YOUR GAUGE.

Polka Dot Ensemble

Delightfully dotty. This elegant ensemble goes from day wear to play wear in no time at all. The demure pink jacket is dressed up with black-bead dots and a tasteful black trim, and comes complete with a ribbed waist that enhances her hourglass figure. Both pieces are knit in cotton in stockinette stitch; the jacket is knit in one piece, requiring only side and sleeve seams for assembly.

jacket

BACK
With A, cast on 20 sts. K 2 rows.
Next row (WS) Change to B and work in St. st until piece measures 2" from beg.

SLEEVE
Next row (RS) Cast on 20 sts, k to end.
Next row (WS) Cast on 20 sts, p to end—60 sts. Work even for 1".
Neckband
Next row (RS) K26 sts, attach new yarn, bind off next 8 sts, k26 sts. Working both sides at once, work 3 rows in St st.

FRONTS
Cast on 2 sts at beg of next 4 rows—30 sts each side for fronts. Cont in St st for ½" more.
Next row (RS) Bind off 20 sts beg of next 2 rows—10 sts each side. Cont in St st until fronts measure same length as back to A. Change to A and k 2 rows.
Next row (RS) With A, k10 sts of right front, pick up 25 sts along right front edge, 32 sts around neck, 25 sts along left front edge, k10 from left front—102 sts. K 1 row. Bind off.

FINISHING
With RS facing and A, pick up and k 21 sts along sleeve edges. K 1 row. Bind off.
Sew side and sleeve seams. Sew beads alternating every 4th st and row.

dress

With A, cast on 40 sts. K 2 rows.
Next row (WS) Work in St st until piece measures 3¼" from beg. Then work in k1, p1 rib for 3 rows.
Next row (WS) Work in St st for 1½". K 2 rows. Bind off.

FINISHING
Sew back seam. Run elastic through ribbing at waist.

materials

Yarn
Knit Cro-Sheen by J & P Coats (approx 150yds/135m) cotton 1 ball each in #12 black (A) and #101 orchid pink (B).
Needles
Size 2 (2.5mm) needles or size needed to obtain gauge
Accessories
Small black beads
Sewing thread
Round black elastic

notes

1 Jacket back, front and sleeves are worked in one piece from the back to the front.
2 Jacket and dress are worked using 2 strands held tog throughout.

gauge

15 sts and 19 rows to 2" over St st using size 2 (2.5mm) needles and Knit Cro-Sheen. FOR PROPER FIT, TAKE THE TIME TO CHECK YOUR GAUGE.

Racing Stripes Sleeveless Pullover and Scarf

Striped lightning. Cruise down the road in style with this of-the-moment striped set. The sleeveless pullover is topped with a matching scarf. A perfect introduction to color striping, both pieces are knit in stripes of candy colors. A fringe benefit: the classy black touch of tuft on the scarf.

Yarn
Paternayan Persian by JCA
(approx 8yd/7.4m) wool
1 skein each of #220 black
(A), #030 blue (B), #670
green (C), #961 pink (D),
#712 yellow (E), #333 lilac
(F), # 263 white (G)
Needles
Sizes 0 and 1 (2 and 2.25mm)
needles or size needed to
obtain gauge
Small crochet hook
Accessories
Small black snap

STRIPE PATTERN

*4 rows F, 4 rows G, 4 rows C, 2
rows A, 4 rows D, 4 rows E, 4 rows
B, 2 rows A; rep from * (28 rows) for
stripe pat.

top

With smaller needles and A, cast on
42 sts. Work in k1, p1 rib for 2 rows.
Work in St st and stripe pat until
piece measures 1½" from beg and 4
rows of D have been worked.
Divide for Front and Backs
Next row (RS) With E, k11 (left
back), k2tog, join another ply of E,
k18 (front), join another ply of E,
k2tog, k to end (right back).
Working all sides at once, cont in St
st and stripe pat until piece
measures approx 3", end k 2 rows A.
Bind off all sts.

FINISHING

Sew shoulder seams. Sew back seam
leaving 1" open at top for neck. Sew
snap at neck edge.

scarf

With A cast on 19 sts. Work in St st
and stripe pat, working 28-row rep
5 times. Piece measures approx
12½". Bind off. With WS tog, sew
long sides of scarf to form tube.
Fringe
Cut 2" lengths of A. With 2 plys held
tog, attach to scarf edges with
crochet hook.

notes

1 Use 1 ply of yarn
throughout.
2 Back and front are worked
in one piece to the underarm.

gauge

8 sts and 11 rows to 1" over
St st using Size 0 (2mm)
needles and 1 ply of yarn.
FOR PROPER FIT, TAKE THE
TIME TO CHECK YOUR GAUGE

Sporty Stripe and Polo Pullover

Here's the pitch! Even a baseball game becomes a fashion show with Barbie pitching style in a cotton striped pullover with a sporty square neck and three-quarter-length sleeves. Her teammate steps up to the plate in a jaunty pullover with preppy polo collar, in red, white, and blue stripes as American as baseball and apple pie. Both are knit in classic stockinette stitch.

sweater for Barbie®

STRIPE PATTERN
*2 rows A, 2 rows B; rep from * (4 rows) for stripe pat.

BACK
With B, beg at lower edge of back and cast on 21 sts. Work in k1, p1 rib for 2 rows. P 1 row. Work in St st and stripe pat until piece measure 2", end with a WS row.
Neck Shaping
Next row (RS) Cont in pat as established, k7, join new yarn and bind off center 7 sts, work to end. Working both sides at once, work even for 1½", end with a WS row.

FRONT
Next row (RS) K7, cast on 7 sts, work to end. Work even in stripe pat, until piece measures same length as back, ending with 2 rows A. Change to B. K 1 row. Work in k1, p1 rib for 2 rows. Bind off in rib.

SLEEVES
Place marker at side edge, 1¾" up from lower edge on front and back. With RS facing and B, pick up and k 20 sts evenly spaced between markers. Beg with B and work in St st and stripe pat, dec 1 st each side every 4th row 3 times—14 sts. Work even until 16 rows of stripes have been completed. Change to B and work in k1, p1 rib for 2 rows. Bind off in rib.

FINISHING
Sew side and sleeve seams.
Neck Edging
With RS facing, crochet hook and B, work a row of sc evenly along front opening. Fasten off.

pullover for Ken®

STRIPE PATTERN
*4 rows B, 4 rows C; rep from * (8 rows) for stripe pat.
BACK
With A, cast on 25 sts. Work in k1, p1 rib for 2 rows. P 1 row. Work in St st and a stripe pat until piece measures 2¼" from beg, end with a WS row. Mark beg and end of next row for armholes. Change to A and work even in St st until piece measures 4" from beg. Bind off.

FRONT
Work as for back until piece measures 3" from beg, end with a WS row.
Front Opening
Next row (RS) K12, join new strand of A and bind off center st, work to end. Working both sides at once with separate strands of A, work even until piece measures 3¾" from beg.
Neck Shaping
Bind off 4 sts at each neck edge. Work even until front measures same length as back. Bind off rem 8 sts each side for shoulders. Sew shoulder seams.

SLEEVES
With RS facing and B, pick up and k 23 sts evenly spaced between armhole markers. Work even in St st for 5 rows. Dec 1 st each side on next row, then every 4th row 3 times more—15 sts. Work even until piece measures 3", end with a WS row. Change to A and p 1 row. Then work 2 rows in k1, p1 rib. Bind off in rib.

FINISHING
Sew side and sleeve seams.
Front Opening Trim
With RS facing, crochet hook and B, work a row of sc evenly along front opening. Fasten off.
Collar
With B, cast on 29 sts. Work in k1, p1 rib for 1". Bind off loosely in rib. Sew collar to neck edge.

SWEATER FOR BARBIE®
Yarn
Matte Tapestry Cotton Art 89 by DMC (approx 11yds/10m) cotton
2 skeins each in white (A) and #2797 blue (B)
Needles
Size 2 (2.5mm) needles or size needed to obtain gauge
Tapestry needle
Size E/4 (3.5mm) crochet hook

PULLOVER FOR KEN®
Yarn
Matte Tapestry Cotton Art 89 by DMC (11yds/10m) cotton
4 skeins #2666 red (B)
2 skeins #2797 blue (A)
1 skein in white (C)

Needles
Size 2 (2.5mm) needles or size needed to obtain gauge
Tapestry needle
Size E/4 (3.5mm) crochet hook

note

SWEATER FOR BARBIE®
Back and front are worked in one piece from back to the front.

gauge

6 sts and 10 rows to 1" over St st using size 2 (2.5mm) needles.
FOR PROPER FIT, TAKE THE TIME TO CHECK YOUR GAUGE.

35

Summer Short Sets

Picnic-perfect.
A trio of cool cotton
short sets brings beauty
to the barbeque. All
three colorful playsuits
are made from the
same basic top-and-
bottom patterns.

red shorts

(make 2)
Beg at waist and with A, cast on 20 sts. Work in k1, p1 rib for 2 rows. Change to B and work in St st until piece measures 2" from beg.
Crotch Shaping
Cast on 2 sts at beg of next 2 rows—24 sts. Work even in St st until piece measures 3" from beg, end with a WS row. Change to A and k 2 rows. Bind off.

FINISHING
Sew front, back and leg seams. Weave 2 strands of elastic thread through ribbing at waist, pull slightly to gather.

red top

With A, cast on 40 sts. K 2 rows. Change to B and work in St st until piece measures 1½" from beg. Bind off.

STRAPS
(make 2)
With B and crochet hook, ch 2".

FINISHING
Sew straps to top at 1" and then 2" in from back edge. Sew snap to upper edge and lower edge of top. Embroider flowers in straight stitch (as show on diagram) with one strand of yarn. Foll photo for color and placement.

hat

With C, cast on 56 sts. K 2 rows. Work in St st for 1".
Crown Shaping
Next (dec) row (RS) K1, *k2tog; rep from *, end k1—29 sts. Cont in St st for ½" more.
Next (dec) row (RS) K1, *k2tog; rep from * to end —15 sts.
Next row (WS) *P2tog; rep from * end p1—8 sts.
Next row *K2tog; rep from * to end—4 sts. Bind off. Pass the 2nd, 3rd and 4th st over the first st. Fasten off.

FINISHING
Sew back seam of hat. With crochet hook and B, work chain-st around hat crown.

reduce diagrams 50% for actual size

RED SET
Yarn
Knit Cro-Sheen by J & P Clark (approx 150yds/135m) cotton 1 each in #001 white (A), #126 red (B), and #123 maize (C)
Small amounts of #182 true blue, #48 green, #10 A canary for embroidery
Needles
Size 3 (3mm) needles or size needed to obtain gauge
Size D/3 (3mm) crochet hook
Accessories
2 snaps
Elastic thread

note

RED SET
1 Work with 2 strands of yarn held tog throughout.
2 Use only one strand of yarn for embroider.

gauge

7 sts and 8 rows to 1" over St st using size 3 (3mm) needles. FOR PROPER FIT, TAKE THE TIME TO CHECK YOUR GAUGE.

Summer Short Sets

Each playsuit is a tube-style top with straps paired with simple shorts—but variations in color, color patterns, and embroidered touches ensure that no two are alike. The rolled-brim hat and tie-back scarf can be made to mix and match with all three sets.

yellow/blue shorts

(make one with A and one with B)
Beg at waist and cast on 20 sts. Work in k1, p1 rib for 2 rows. Then work in St st until piece measures 2" from beg.

Crotch Shaping
Cast on 2 sts at beg of next 2 rows—24 sts. Work even in St st until piece measures 3" from beg, end with a WS row. K 2 rows. Bind off.

FINISHING
Sew front, back and leg seams. Weave 2 strands of elastic thread through ribbing at waist, pull slightly to gather.

yellow/blue top

Cast on 20 sts with A, 20 sts with B. Work in St st for 2". Bind off.

FINISHING
Sew snap to upper and lower edges of top.
Tie
With crochet hook and A, ch 8". Fold in half and sew center of ch to center front.

blue kerchief

Cast on 47 sts.
Next row Bind off 11 sts, k to last 11 sts, bind off 11 sts. Break yarn. Attach yarn and k 1 row, p 1 row.
Next row (RS) Ssk, k to last 3 sts, k2tog, k1. P 1 row.
Rep last 2 rows 9 times more—5 sts.
Next row K1, SK2P, k1—3 sts.
Next row SK2P.
Fasten off.

green shorts

(make 2)
Beg at waist and with A, cast on 20 sts. Work in k1, p1 rib for 2 rows. Change to B and work in St st until piece measures 2" from beg.
Crotch Shaping
Cast on 2 sts at beg of next 2 rows—24 sts. Work even in St st until piece measures 3" from beg, end with a WS row. Change to A and k 2 rows. Bind off.

FINISHING
Sew front, back and leg seams. Weave 2 strands of elastic thread through ribbing at waist, pull slightly to gather.

green top

With A, cast on 40 sts. K 2 rows. Change to B and work even in St st for 6 rows.
Next row (RS) *K2 B, k2 A; rep from * to end.
Next row *K2 A, k2 B; rep from * to end.
With A, work 4 rows in St st.
Next row (RS) *K2 B, k2 A; rep from * to end.
Next row *K2 A, k2 B; rep from * to end.
K 2 rows with B. Bind off.

STRAPS
(make 2)
With B and crochet hook, ch 2".

FINISHING
Sew straps to top at 1" and then 2" in from back edge. Sew snap to upper edge and lower edge of top.

materials

YELLOW/BLUE SET
Yarn
Knit Cro-Sheen by J & P Clark (approx 150yds/135m) cotton 1 ball each in #182 true blue (A) and #10A canary (B)
Needles
Size 3 (3mm) needles or size needed to obtain gauge
Size D/3 (3mm) crochet hook
Accessories
2 snaps
Elastic thread
GREEN SET
Yarn
Knit Cro-Sheen by J & P Clark (approx 150yds/137m) cotton 1 each in #182 true Blue (A) and #48 green (B)
Needles
Size 3 (3mm) needles or size needed to obtain gauge
Size D/3 (3mm) crochet hook
Accessories
2 snaps
Elastic thread

notes

YELLOW/BLUE SET
When changing colors, twist yarns on WS to prevent holes.
GREEN SET
Work with 2 strands of yarn held tog throughout.

gauge

7 sts and 8 rows to 1" over St st using size 3 (3mm) needles . FOR PROPER FIT, TAKE THE TIME TO CHECK YOUR GAUGE.

Windbreaker, Baseball and Denim Jackets

Jacket jive.
No matter what the
activity, Barbie® has the
jacket to match—be
it a colorful hooded
windbreaker, a baseball-
style jacket, or a
go-with-everything
denim classic. All
three feature a basic
button-front style in
stockinette stitch, and
all have identical
shaping—the difference
is in the details.

WINDBREAKER
Yarn
Paternayan Persian by JCA
(approx 8yd/7.4m) wool
2 skeins in #962 pink (A)
1 skein each #592 turquoise
(B), #760 yellow (C),
#811 orange (D), and
#670 green (E)
Needles
Size 2 (2.5mm) needles or
size needed to obtain gauge
Tapestry needle
Size C/2 (2.5mm) crochet
hook
Accessories
7 turquoise beads

windbreaker

BACK

With A cast on 19 sts. Work in k1,
p1 rib for 2 rows.
Next row (RS) K, inc 3 sts evenly
spaced—22 sts. Cont in St st until
piece measures 3" from beg.
Armhole Shaping
Bind off 2 sts at beg of next 2
rows—18 sts. Work even until piece
measures 4¼" from beg. Bind off.

LEFT FRONT

With B, cast on 9 sts. Work in k1, p1
rib for 2 rows.
Next row (RS) K, inc 2 sts evenly
space—11 sts. Cont in St st until
piece measures 3" from beg.
Armhole Shaping
Next row (RS) Bind off 2 sts, work
to end—9 sts. Work even until piece
measures 4" from beg, end with a
RS row.
Neck Shaping
Next row (WS) Bind off 1 st at neck
edge, work to end. Cont to bind off
1 st at neck edge 3 times more—5
sts. Work even until front measures
same length as back to shoulders.
Bind off.

RIGHT FRONT

With C, cast on 9 sts. Work as for
left front, reversing all shaping.

notes

ALL JACKETS
1 Use 2 plys of yarn held
tog throughout.
2 Use 1 ply of yarn to
sew seams.

gauge

7 sts and 9 rows to 1" over St
st. using size 2 (2.5mm)
needles and 2 plys of yarn
held tog.
FOR PROPER FIT, TAKE THE
TIME TO CHECK YOUR GAUGE.

Windbreaker, Baseball and Denim Jackets

The windbreaker is knit a bit longer, in contrasting colors with a drawstring hood attached. Her baseball jacket is worked in pink with white sleeves, contrasting trim, and the essential embroidered initial. The denim jacket is topstitched with gold for a real jean-jacket look.

SLEEVE
(make 1 in D, 1 in E)
Cast on 10 sts. Work in k1, p1 rib for 2 rows.
Next row (RS) K, inc 1 st each side on this row, then every 4th row 4 times more—20 sts. Work even until piece measures 3" from beg. Bind off.

FINISHING
Sew shoulder seams. Set in sleeves. Sew side and sleeve seams.
Front Band
With RS facing and A, pick up and k 31 sts evenly along left front edge. Work in k1, p1 rib for 2 rows. Bind off loosely in rib. Rep for right front.
Embroidery
With A, embroider a mock slash pocket in chain-stitch on both fronts.
Sew on 7 turquoise beads evenly spaced along left front.

hood

With A, cast on 39 sts. Work in k1, p1 rib for 3 rows. Work in St st until piece measures 2" from beg. Bind off. Fold in half and sew bound-off edge tog. Sew hood around neck edge.
Tie
With A and crochet hook, ch 12". Fasten off. Weave chain through ribbing on hood. Knot each end.

baseball jacket

BACK
With A cast on 19 sts. Work in k1, p1 rib for 4 rows.

Next row (RS) K, inc 3 sts evenly spaced—22 sts.
Cont in St st until piece measures 2½" from beg.
Armhole Shaping
Bind off 2 sts at beg of next 2 rows—18 sts. Work even until piece measures 3½" from beg. Bind off.

LEFT FRONT
With A, cast on 9 sts. Work in k1, p1 rib for 4 rows.
Next row (RS) K, inc 2 sts evenly spaced—11 sts.
Cont in St st until piece measures 2½" from beg.
Armhole Shaping
Next row (RS) Bind off 2 sts, work to end—9 sts. Work even until piece measures 3" from beg, end with a RS row.
Neck Shaping
Next row (WS) Bind off 1 st at neck edge, work to end. Cont to bind off 1 st at neck edge 3 times more—5 sts. Work even until front measures same length as back to shoulders. Bind off.

RIGHT FRONT
Work as for left front, reversing all shaping.

SLEEVE
With A cast on 10 sts. Work in k1, p1 rib for 2 rows. Change to B and work in St st, inc 1 st each side on this row, then every 8th row twice more—16 sts. Work even until piece measures 3" from beg. Bind off.

FINISHING
Sew shoulder seams. Set in sleeves. Sew side and sleeve seams.

Front Band

With RS facing and A, pick up and k 24 sts evenly along left front edge. Work in k1, p1 rib for 2 rows. Bind off loosely in rib. Rep for right front.

Neckband

With RS facing and A, pick up and k 25 sts evenly spaced around neck edge, including front bands. Work in k1, p1, rib for 4 rows. Bind off loosely in rib.

Embroidery

With B, embroider a mock slash pocket in chain-stitch on both fronts.

Sew on 6 buttons evenly spaced along left front band.

denim jacket

BACK

With A cast on 19 sts. Work in k1, p1 rib for 4 rows.

Next row (RS) K, inc 3 sts evenly spaced—22 sts.

Cont in St st until piece measures 2½" from beg.

Armhole Shaping

Bind off 2 sts at beg of next 2 rows—18 sts. Work even until piece measures 3½" from beg. Bind off.

LEFT FRONT

With A, cast on 9 sts. Work in k1, p1 rib for 4 rows.

Next row (RS) K, inc 2 sts evenly spaced—11 sts.

Cont in St st until piece measures 2½" from beg.

Armhole Shaping

Next row (RS) Bind off 2 sts, work to end—9 sts. Work even until piece measures 3" from beg, end with a RS row.

Neck Shaping

Next row (WS) Bind off 1 st at neck edge, work to end. Cont to bind off 1 st at neck edge 3 times more—5 sts. Work even until front measures same length as back to shoulders. Bind off

RIGHT FRONT

Work as for left front, reversing all shaping.

SLEEVE

With A, cast on 10 sts. Work in k1, p1 rib for 2 rows.

Next row (RS) K, inc 1 st each side. Cont in St st, inc 1 st each side every 4th row 4 times more—20 sts. Work even until piece measures 3" from beg. Bind off.

FINISHING

Sew shoulder seams. Set in sleeves. Sew side and sleeve seams.

Front Band

With RS facing and A, pick up and k 24 sts evenly spaced along left front edge. Work in k1, p1 rib for 2 rows. Bind off loosely in rib. Rep for right front.

Collar

With RS facing and A, pick up and k 25 sts evenly spaced along neck edge, including front bands. Work in k1, p1, rib for 1". Bind off loosely in rib.

Embroidery

With B, embroider a row of running stitches above rib along the lower edge body and sleeves. On each front, embroider a "V" using running stitch (see photo on page 40). Sew on 6 yellow beads for buttons, evenly spaced along left front.

materials

BASEBALL JACKET

Yarn

Paternayan Persian by JCA (approx 8yd/7.4m) wool
3 skeins in #962 pink (A)
2 skeins #260 white (B)

Needles

Size 2 (2.5mm) needles or size needed to obtain gauge
Tapestry needle

Accessories

6 buttons JHB #13055 in white

DENIM JACKET

Yarn

Paternayan Persian by JCA (approx 8yd/7.4m) wool
4 skeins of #542 blue (A)
1 skein #710 gold (B)

Needles

Size 2 (2.5mm) needles or size needed to obtain gauge
Tapestry needle

Accessories

6 yellow beads

notes

ALL JACKETS

1 Use 2 plys of yarn held tog throughout.
2 Use 1 ply of yarn to sew seams.

gauge

7 sts and 9 rows to 1" over St st using size 2 (2.5mm) needles and 2 plies of yarn held tog.
FOR PROPER FIT, TAKE THE TIME TO CHECK YOUR GAUGE.

Car Coat, Anorak and Pea Coat

Haute coat–ure. When autumn leaves start to fall, fashion goes outdoors, and these coat choices boast good taste down to the smallest detail. All are knit in stockinette stitch with tapestry wool—perfectly finished down to their folded-up hems. The tan car coat sports a hood, patch pockets, and real toggle closings.

car coat

BACK
Cast on 24 sts. Work in St st for 3 rows. K next row on WS for turning ridge. Cont in St st until piece measures 4" above turning ridge.
Armhole Shaping
Bind off 4 sts at beg of next 2 rows—16 sts. Work even until armhole measures 1½". Bind off.

LEFT FRONT
Cast on 15 sts. Work as for back, working armhole shaping at beg of RS row only—11 sts. Work even until armhole measures 1", end with a RS row.
Neck Shaping
Next row (WS) Bind off 4 sts, work to end. K 1 row. Dec 1 st at neck edge on next row—6 sts. Work even until piece measures same length as back. Bind off.

RIGHT FRONT
Work to correspond to left front, reversing all shaping.

SLEEVES
Cast on 14 sts. Work in k1, p1 rib for 2 rows. Work in St st, inc 1 st each side every 4th row 3 times—20 sts. Work even until piece measures 3" from beg. Bind off.

HOOD
Cast on 39 sts. Work in k1, p1 rib for 2 rows. Then work in St st until piece measures 2" from beg. Bind off. Fold in half with WS tog, and sew bound-off edge tog for back seam.

materials

CAR COAT
Yarn
Paternayan Persian by JCA (approx 8yd/7.4m) wool
7 skeins in #443 camel
Needles
Size 2 (2.5mm) needles or size needed to obtain gauge
Size C/2 (2.5mm) crochet hook
Accessories
3 JHB #92999 ¼" golden ball buttons

note

ALL JACKETS
Use 2 plys of yarn held tog throughout.

gauge

7 sts and 9 rows to 1" over St st using size 2 (2.5mm) needles and 2 plys of yarn held tog.
FOR PROPER FIT, TAKE THE TIME TO CHECK YOUR GAUGE.

The green anorak is topped with a delightfully impish hood and is cinched at the waist with a crocheted drawstring. The navy pea coat—ever a classic with a neat collar, and patch pockets.

POCKET

(make 2)
Cast on 8 sts. Work in St st for 1". Bind off. Sew pockets to fronts, 1½" above turning ridge and ½" in from front edge.

FINISHING

Sew shoulder seams. Set in sleeves. Sew sleeves between markers. Sew side and sleeve seams. Turn hem to WS at turning ridge and sew in place. Beg at ½" in from front edge and sew hood around neck.

Front Edging

With RS facing and crochet hook, work a row of sc evenly along left front edge. Fasten off. Rep for right front.

Button Loops

On right front edge, embroider a horizontal row of chain sts, ¼" down from neck edge and 1" in from edge. With crochet hook, make a 1" chain for the button loop. Fold button loop in half and sew to front edge at embroidered chain-sts. Rep twice more spaced 1" apart. Sew gold ball buttons to left front edge opposite button loops.

anorak

BACK

Cast on 24 sts. Work in St st for 3 rows. K next row on WS for turning ridge. Cont in St st until piece measures 3¼" above turning ridge.

Armhole Shaping

Bind off 4 sts at beg of next 2 rows—16 sts. Work even until armhole measures 1½". Bind off.

LEFT FRONT

Cast on 15 sts. Work as for back, working armhole shaping at beg of RS row only—11 sts. Work even until armhole measures 1", end with a RS row.

Neck Shaping

Next row (WS) Bind off 4 sts, work to end. K 1 row. Dec 1 st at neck edge on next row—6 sts. Work even until piece measures same length as back. Bind off.

RIGHT FRONT

Work to correspond to left front, reversing all shaping.

SLEEVES

Cast on 14 sts. Work in k1, p1 rib for 2 rows. Work in St st, inc 1 st each side every 4th row 3 times—20 sts. Work even until piece measures 3" from beg. Bind off.

HOOD

Cast on 39 sts. Work in k1, p1 rib for 2 rows. Then work in St st until piece measures 2" from beg. Bind off. Fold in half with WS tog, and sew bound-off edge tog for back seam.

FINISHING

Sew shoulder seams. Set in sleeves. Sew sleeves between markers. Sew side and sleeve seams. Beg at ½" in from front edge and sew hood around neck.

Front Edging

With RS facing and crochet hook, work a row of sc evenly along left front edge. Fasten off. Rep for right front.
Turn hem to WS at turning ridge and sew in place, leaving open at front edge for casing.

Pockets

Embroider a mock slash pocket with a diagonal chain-st on each front.

Waist Tie

With crochet hook, chain 12" for tie. Beg at 2" from lower edge and weave tie over and under every 2 sts around waist. Knot tie ends.

Bottom Tie

With crochet hook, chain 12½" for tie. Thread through casing. Trim and knot ends.

pea coat

BACK

Cast on 24 sts. Work in St st for 3 rows. K next row on WS for turning ridge. Cont in St st until piece measures 3" above turning ridge.

Armhole Shaping

Bind off 4 sts at beg of next 2 rows—16 sts. Work even until armhole measures 1½". Bind off.

LEFT FRONT

Cast on 15 sts. Work as for back, working armhole shaping at beg of RS row only. Work even until armhole measures 1", end with a RS row.

Neck Shaping

Next row (WS) Bind off 4 sts, work to end. K 1 row. Dec 1 st at neck edge on next row—6 sts. Work even until piece measures same length as back. Bind off.

RIGHT FRONT

Work to correspond to left front, reversing all shaping.

SLEEVES

Cast on 14 sts. Work in k1, p1 rib for 2 rows. Work in St st, inc 1 st each side every 4th row 3 times—20 sts. Work even until piece measures 3" from beg. Bind off.

POCKET

(make 2)

Cast on 8 sts. Work in St st for 1". Bind off. Sew pockets to fronts, 1½" above turning ridge and ½" in from front edge.

FINISHING

Sew shoulder seams. Set in sleeves. Sew sleeves between markers. Sew side and sleeve seams. Turn hem to WS at turning ridge and sew in place.

Front Edging

With RS facing and crochet hook, work a row of sc evenly along left front edge. Fasten off. Rep for right front.

Collar

With WS facing, beg and end at ½" in from front edges and pick up and k 18 sts evenly spaced around neck. Beg with a k row and work in reverse St st for 1¼". Bind off. Sew beads to left front for buttons.

materials

ANORAK

Yarn

Paternayan Persian by JCA (approx 8yd/7.4m) wool
7 skeins in #692 green

Needles

Size 2 (2.5mm) needles or size to needed to obtain gauge
Size C/2 (2.5mm) crochet hook

PEA COAT

Yarn

Paternayan Persian by JCA (approx 8yd/7.4m) wool
ß6 skeins in #501 navy

Needles

Size 2 (2.5mm) needles or size to needed to obtain gauge
Size C/2 (2.5mm) crochet hook

Accessories

Four ⅛"/3mm blue beads

note

ALL JACKETS

Use 2 plys of yarn held tog throughout.

gauge

7 sts and 9 rows to 1" over St st using size 2 (2.5mm) needles and 2 plys of yarn held tog.
FOR PROPER FIT, TAKE THE TIME TO CHECK YOUR GAUGE.

Summer Party Dresses

The three Graces. Joy, beauty, and bloom abound in these sophisticated summer dresses, sure to be seen at the best parties of the season. All three dresses are the same in style—daringly shoulder-baring with close-fitting necklines, dainty shaped waists, and blossoming full skirts—but vary in hemline, color, and detail.

blue dress

STRIPE PATTERN
Work in St st as foll; *2 rows B, 2 rows A; rep from * (4 rows) for stripe pat.

SKIRT
With A, cast on 74 sts. K 1 row on WS, then work in St st until piece measures 4" from beg, end with WS row.
Next row (RS) K1, *k3tog; rep from *, end k1—26 sts.

BODICE
Work 3 rows in St st (for waist), end with a WS row.
Next row (RS) Change to B, work in stripe pat and bind off 3 sts at beg of next 2 rows—20 sts.
Next (dec) row (RS) K1, ssk, k to last 3 sts, k2tog, k1. Work 3 rows even.
Rep last 4 rows 4 times more. Change to B and work dec row once—8 sts. P 1 row.
Neckband
Next row (RS) Change to A and cast on 6 sts at beg of next 2 rows—20 sts. P 1 row, k 1 row. Bind off.

FINISHING
Sew back seam, leaving open 1½" down from waist. Sew snap to waist and to neckband

BLUE DRESS
Yarn
Knit Cro-Sheen by J & P Coats (approx150yds/137m) cotton 1 ball in #180 delft blue (A) Small amount in #10A canary yellow (B)
Needles
Size 3 (3mm) needles or size needed to obtain gauge
Accessories
2 small snaps
WHITE DRESS
Yarn
Knit Cro-Sheen by J & P Coats (approx 150yds/137m) cotton 1 ball in #001 white (A) Small amounts of #168 jade (B) and #46A midrose (C)
Needles
Size 3 (3mm) needles or size to obtain gauge
Tapestry needle
Accessories
2 small snaps

note

ALL DRESSES
Work with 2 strands of yarn held tog throughout.

gauge

7 sts and 8 rows to 1" over St st using size 3 (3mm) needles and 2 strands of yarn held tog.
FOR PROPER FIT, TAKE THE TIME TO CHECK YOUR GAUGE.

Summer Party Dresses

The knee-length blue dress is striped with yellow at the bodice, while the short white frock features pink lazy-daisy stitch flowers with green detail and a matching green garter-stitch hem. The third gown is solid pink with a delicately embroidered floral hem and a single flower centered at the neck front. All are knit in stockinette with crisp cotton.

white dress

SKIRT
With B, cast on 74 sts. K 1 row on WS, Change to A and work in St st until piece measures 3" from beg, end with WS row.
Next row (RS) K1, *k3tog; rep from *, end k1—26 sts.

BODICE
Work 3 rows in St st (for waist).
Next row (RS) Bind off 3 sts at beg of next 2 rows—20 sts.
Next (dec) row (RS) K1, ssk, k to last 3 sts, end k2tog, k1. Work 3 rows even.
Rep last 4 rows 4 times. Work dec row—8 sts. P 1 row.
Neckband
Next row (RS) Cast on 6 sts at beg of next 2 rows—20 sts. P 1 row, k 1 row. Bind off.

FINISHING
Sew back seam, leaving open 1½" down from waist. Sew snap to waist and to neckband.
Embroidery
Work flowers, foll diagram, around skirt and on bodice.

pink dress

SKIRT
With B, cast on 74 sts. K 1 row on WS, then work in St st for ½". Change to A and cont in St st until piece measures 4½" form beg, end with WS row.
Next row (RS) K1, *k3tog; rep from *, end k1—26 sts.

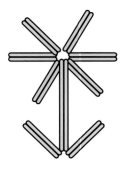

Reduce diagrams 50% for actual size.

BODICE

Work 3 rows in St st (for waist).

Next row (RS) Bind off 3 sts at beg of next 2 rows—20 sts.

Next (dec) row (RS) K1, ssk, k to last 3 sts, end k2tog, k1. Work 3 rows even.

Rep last 4 rows 4 times. Work dec row—8 sts. P 1 row.

Neckband

Next row (RS) Cast on 6 sts at beg of next 2 rows—20 sts. P 1 row, k 1 row. Bind off.

FINISHING

Sew back seam, leaving open 1½" down from waist. Sew snap to waist and to neckband.

Embroidery

Work flowers, foll diagram, around lower edge and on bodice.

materials

PINK DRESS

Yarn

Knit Cro-Sheen by J & P Coats (approx150yds/137m) cotton 1 ball in #101 orchid pink (A) Small amount of #001 white (B) purple, green and yellow for embroidery

Needles

Size 3 (3mm) needles or size needed to obtain gauge Tapestry needle

Accessories

2 small snaps

note

Work with 2 strands of yarn held tog throughout.

gauge

7 sts and 8 rows to 1" over St st using size 3 (3mm) needles and 2 stands of yarn held tog. FOR PROPER FIT, TAKE THE TIME TO CHECK YOUR GAUGE.

Fabulous Faux Fur Coats

Faux, glorious faux. These leopard and lamb "fur" coats and hats are smart choices for high-style winter wear. The spots on the leopard coat are worked in a duplicate stitch after the piece has been knit in stockinette, and the garter-stitch collar and trim fairly purr with texture and contrast.

leopard coat

BACK
With A cast on 22 sts. Work in St st until piece measures 4¼" from beg, end with a WS row.

Armhole Shaping
Bind off 4 sts at beg of next 2 rows—14 sts. Work even until armhole measures 1½". Bind off.

LEFT FRONT
With A cast on 11 sts. Work in St st until piece measures 4¼" from beg, end with a WS.

Armhole Shaping
Next row (RS) Bind off 3 sts, work to end—8 sts. Work even until armhole measures 1", end with a RS row.

Neck Shaping
Next row (WS) Bind off 3 sts, work to end—5 sts. Work even until armhole measures 1½". Bind off.

RIGHT FRONT
Work to correspond to left front, reversing all shaping.

SLEEVES
With B, cast on 12 sts. Work in garter st (k every row) for ½". Change to A and work in St st, inc 1 st each side every 4th row 3 times—18 sts. Work even until piece measures 3" from beg. Bind off.

FINISHING
Embroider spots on back, fronts and sleeves foll chart using duplicate stitch.
With sewing needle and matching thread, sew shoulder seams.

Collar
With RS facing and B, cast on 24 sts. Work in garter st for 1". Bind off. Sew collar around neck edge.

Left Front Band
With B, pick up and k 31 sts evenly spaced along left front. K 2 rows. Bind off. Rep for right front.
With sewing needle and matching thread, set in sleeves. Sew side and sleeve seams. Sew beads evenly spaced along left front.

Color Key
☐ Tan A

● Dk Brown B

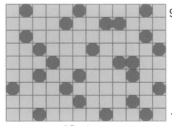

12-st rep

Yarn
Tiny Tresses by Twice As Nice Design, Ltd. (approx 38yds/35m) cotton
2 balls #322 tan (A)
1 ball #324 dark brown (B)

Needles
Size 2 (2.5mm) needles or size needed to obtain gauge
Tapestry needle
Sewing needle.

Accessories
Sewing thread
Gold beads for buttons

note
Spots are worked in duplicate stitch on finished pieces.

gauge
13 sts and 17 rows to 2" over St st using size 2 (2.5mm) needles.
FOR PROPER FIT, TAKE THE TIME TO CHECK YOUR GAUGE.

Fabulous Faux Fur Coats

The nubby yarn used for the lamb coat creates a natural look when knit in reverse stockinette, and the garter-stitch cuffs and rolled front give the coat a flattering dimension. Matching hats complete the sumptuous look.

leopard hat

With B cast on 28 sts. Work in garter st for 1", end with a WS row. Change to A.
Next row (RS) K, dec 4 sts evenly spaced—24 sts. Work 3 rows in St st.
Next row (RS) K1, *k2tog; rep from *, end k1—13 sts. P 1 row.
Next row K1, *k2tog; rep from * to end—7 sts. Draw yarn through rem sts. Pull tightly to gather.

FINISHING

With B, embroider spots using duplicate stitch, foll chart on page 53.
With sewing needle and thread, sew back seam.

persian lamb coat

BACK

Cast on 22 sts. Work in reverse St st until piece measures 5½" from beg, end with a WS row.
Armhole Shaping
Bind off 4 sts at beg of next 2 rows—14 sts. Work even until armholes measure 1½". Bind off.

LEFT FRONT

Cast on 13 sts. Work in reverse St st until piece measures 5½" from beg, end with a WS row.

Armhole Shaping
Next row (RS) Bind off 3 sts, work to end—10 sts. Work even until armhole measures 1½", end with a WS row.
Shawl Collar Shaping
Bind off 5 sts at beg of next row—5 sts. Work even in rev St st over 5 sts for ½". Bind off.

RIGHT FRONT

Work to correspond to left front, reversing all shaping.

SLEEVES

Cast on 12 sts. Work in reverse St st, inc 1 st each side every 4th row 3 times—18 sts. Work even until sleeve measures 3½" from beg.
Bind off.

FINISHING

Using sewing needle and matching thread, sew shoulder seams. Set in sleeves. Sew side and sleeve seams. Sew bound-off edges of collar tog and sew to neck edge. Fold back sleeves for cuffs.

Yarn
Tiny Tresses by Twice As Nice
Design, Ltd. (approx
38yds/35m) cotton
3 balls in #325 terra cotta
Needles
Size 2 (2.5mm) needles
or size needed to
obtain gauge
Tapestry needle
Sewing needle
Accessories
Match sewing thread

persian lamb hat

Cast on 28 sts.
Work in garter st for 1".
Next row (RS) Work in St st, dec 4
sts evenly spaced—24 sts. Work 3
rows in St st.
Next row (RS) K1, *k2tog; rep
from *, end k1—13 sts. P 1 row.
Next row K1, *k2tog; rep from *
to end—7 sts. Draw yarn through
rem sts. Pull tightly to gather. Sew
back seam.

gauge

13 sts and 17 rows to 2" over
St st using size 2 (2.5mm)
needles.
FOR PROPER FIT, TAKE THE
TIME TO CHECK YOUR
GAUGE.

Classic Argyle and XO Pullovers

Hugs and kisses.
Puppy love or best of
friends? Either way,
these two—and their
canine pals—share
oodles of cuddles
in these
traditionally
patterned pullovers.
His X's and O's are
worked using a
Fair Isle
technique—the unused
colors are carried across
the back.

pullover for Ken®

STRIPE PATTERN

*2 rows B, 6 rows A; rep from * (8 rows) for stripe pat.

BACK

With A, cast on 25 sts. Work in k1, p1 rib for 2 rows. Work 4 rows in St st. Then work in St st and stripe pat until piece measures 2¾" from beg, end with 2 rows B.

Armhole Shaping

With A, bind off 3 sts at beg of next 2 rows—19 sts.
Work even for ¾" more.

Neck Opening

Next row (RS) K9, join another 2 plys of A and bind off 1 st, work to end. Cont in St st with A only until piece measures 4¾" from beg. Bind off.

Color Key
■ Cranberry A
○ White B

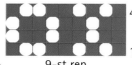

4
1
9-st rep

FRONT

Work as for back (omit neck opening) until piece measures 4" from beg.

Neck Shaping

K7, join another 2 plys of A and bind off center 5 sts, work to end. Working both sides at once, dec 1 st at each neck edge on next RS row— 6 sts each side. Work even with A only until piece measures same length as back. Bind off.

SLEEVES

With A, cast on 14 sts. Work in St st and stripe pat, inc 1 st each side every 4th row 3 times—20 sts. Work even until piece measures 3½" from beg. Bind off.

FINISHING

With 2 plys of B, foll chart and duplicate st "X" and "O" on front and sleeves (see photo).
Weave A through center of B stripe on back.

Neckband

Sew shoulder seams. With RS facing and A, pick up and k 25 sts around neck edge. Work in k1, p1 rib for 2 rows. Bind off.
Set in sleeves. Sew side and sleeve seams. Sew snap to back neck.

materials

PULLOVER FOR KEN®
Yarn
Patemayan Persian by JCA (approx 8yd/7.4m) wool
5 skeins in #940 cranberry (A)
2 skeins in #948 white (B)
Needles
Size 3 (3mm) needles or size needed to obtain gauge
Accessories
1 snap
Tapestry needle
DOG SWEATER
Yarn
Patemayan Persian by JCA (8yds/7.4m) wool
1 skein each in #940 cranberry (A), 1 skein of #948 pale pink (B)
Needles
Size 3 (3mm) or size needed to obtain gauge

notes

1 Use 2 plys of yarn held tog throughout.
2 X and O's are worked in duplicate st, foll chart.

gauge

6 sts and 8 rows to 1" over St st using size 2 (2.5mm) needles 2 plys of yarn held tog.
FOR PROPER FIT, TAKE THE TIME TO CHECK YOUR GAUGE.

Classic Argyle and XO Pullovers

Her argyle look is knit in green and white stockinette stripes, then embroidered with red backstitched diamonds. The dogs' sweaters pick up the patterns of their human companions.

dog sweater

With A, beg at neck and cast on 26 sts. Work in k1, p1 rib for 3 rows. P 1 row.

Next row (RS) K1, ssk, k to last 3 sts, k2tog, k1—24 sts. P 1 row. Rep last 2 rows until piece measures 1½" from beg. Cont to rep last 2 rows, AT SAME TIME, work stripe pat, then work 2 rows B, 6 rows A, 2 rows B, then cont with A to end of piece—8 sts.

Next row K2tog, bind off to last 2 sts, k2tog and bind off.

FINISHING

With 2 plys of B, foll chart and duplicate st "X" and "O" foll chart on page 57. Sew rib tog for back seam.

Strap

With A pick up 5 sts on right side, 1¼" from cast-on edge and work in k1, p1 rib for 2½". Bind off. Sew to opposite side.

sweater for Barbie®

STRIPE PATTERN

*4 rows A, 4 rows B; rep from * (8 rows) for stripe pat.

BACK

With C, cast on 20 sts. Work in k1, p1 rib for 2 rows. Work in St st and stripe pat until piece measures 4" from beg. Bind off.

FRONT

Work as for back until piece measures 3½" from beg, end with a WS row.

Neck shaping

K7, join yarn and bind off center 6 sts, work to end. Working both sides at once, dec 1 st at each neck edge every other row twice—5 sts each side. Work even until piece measures same length as back. Bind off 5 sts each side.

SLEEVES

With C, cast on 10 sts. Work in k1, p1 rib for 2 rows. Change to A and work in St st, inc 1 st each side on next row, then every 4th row 3 times—18 sts. Work even until piece measures 3" from beg. Bind off.

FINISHING

With 2 plys of C, embroider diamonds on front, foll photo. Sew shoulder seams.

Neckband

With C cast on 28 sts. Work in k1, p1 rib for 4 rows. Bind off in rib. Sew back seam of neckband. Sew neckband along neck edge centering back seam at center back neck edge. Place marker 1½" down from shoulders on front and back. Sew sleeves between markers. Sew side and sleeve seams.

dog sweater

With C, beg at neck and cast on 22 sts. Work in k1, p1 rib for 2 rows. P 1 row.

Next row (RS) K1, ssk, k to last 3 sts, k2tog, k1—20 sts. P 1 row. Rep last 2 rows once more. Beg stripe pat and cont to rep last 2 rows 5 times more—8 sts.

Next row K2tog, bind off to last 2 sts, k2tog and bind off.

FINISHING

With 2 plys of C, embroider diamonds as for front. Sew rib tog for back seam.

Strap

With A, pick up 5 sts on right side, 1¼" from cast-on edge and work in k1, p1 rib for 2½". Bind off. Sew to opposite side.

SWEATER FOR BARBIE®

Yarn

Paternayan Persian by JCA (approx 8yd/7.4m) wool
3 skeins in #640 green (A)
2 skeins #263 cream (B)
1 skein in #968 red (C)

Needles

Size 2 (2.5mm) needles or size needed to obtain gauge
Tapestry needle

DOG SWEATER

Yarn

Paternayan Persian by JCA (approx 8yd/7.4m) wool
1 skein each in #640 green (A), #968 red (C), and #263 cream (B)

Needles

Size 2 (2.5mm) needles or size needed to obtain gauge

Accessories

Tapestry needle

note

Use 2 plys of yarn held tog throughout.

gauge

6 sts and 9 rows to 1" over St st using size 3 (3mm) needles and 2 plys of yarn held tog. FOR PROPER FIT, TAKE THE TIME TO CHECK YOUR GAUGE.

Scandinavian Ski Sets

The hills are alive. Whether it's her effortless maneuvering over moguls, her fearless sheer drops, or her impeccable ski suits, Barbie® will be the center of attention on the slopes. The blue ski set features a stockinette sweater trimmed with white and embroidered with a Scandinavian snowflake pattern.

blue sweater

With B, cast on 38 sts. Work in k1, p1 rib for 2 rows. K 1 row.

Next row (WS) Change to A and cont in St st until piece measures 1½" from beg, end with a RS row.
Next row (WS) With B, p 1 row.
Next row *K3 B, k1 A; rep from *, end k2 B. Change to A and work 7 rows in St st.
Next row *K3 B, k1 A; rep from *, end k2 B. With B, p 1 row.**
Divide for Front and Backs
Change to A and k8 (left back), bind off 2 sts, k18 (front), bind off 2 sts, k8 (right back).

RIGHT BACK

Next row (WS) P8, sl rem sts to holder. Work even in St st for 2 rows.
Next (dec) row K1, k2tog, work to end—7 sts. P 1 row.
Rep last 2 rows 3 times more—4 sts. Sl to holder.

FRONT

P next 18 sts from holder. Work in St st for 2 rows.
Next (dec) row K1, k2tog, k to last 3 sts, k2tog k1—16 sts. P 1 row.
Rep last 2 rows 3 times more—10 sts. Sl to holder.

LEFT BACK

P last 8 sts from holder. Work even in St st for 2 rows.
Next (dec) row K to last 3 sts, k2tog, k1—7 sts. P 1 row.
Rep last 2 rows 3 times more—4 sts. Sl to holder.

SLEEVES

With B, cast on 10 sts. Work in k1, p1 rib for 2 rows. K 1 row.
Next row (WS) Change to A and work in St st until piece measures 1½" from beg, then work from ** to ** as for back, AT THE SAME TIME, inc 1 st each side every 4th row 4 times—18 sts. Work even until piece measures 3" from beg.

Raglan Shaping
Bind off 2 sts at beg of next 2 rows.
Next (dec) row K1, k2tog, k to last 3 sts, k2tog, k1. P 1 row.
Rep last 2 rows 4 times more—4 sts. Sl to holder.

FINISHING

Embroidery
With 2 plys of B, straight stitch snowflakes on color band, 3 on front and 2 on back, follow diagram. Embroider a snowflake in center of color band on sleeves.
Sew raglan seams, then sew sleeve seams.
Mock Turtleneck
With RS facing, sl sts from holders to needle—26 sts. With B, k 1 row, then work in k1, p1 rib for 3 rows. Bind off loosely in rib.
Sew back seam, leaving top 1½" open at neck. Sew snap at turtleneck.

blue ski pants

(make 2 pieces)
Beg at waist, with A cast on 18 sts. Work in k1, p1 rib for 2 rows. Work in St st until piece measures 2" from beg.
Crotch Shaping
Cast on 2 sts at beg of next 2 rows—22 sts. Work even for 1½".
Leg Shaping
Dec 1 st at beg of next 2 rows, then every 6th row 3 times more—14 sts. Work even until piece measures 6½" from beg. Bind off.

BLUE SET
Yarn
Paternayan Persian by JCA (approx 8yd/7.4m) wool
7 skeins in #583 sky blue (A)
2 skeins in #261 cream (B)
Needles
Size 3 (3mm) needles or size needed to obtain gauge
Size B/1 (2mm) crochet hook
Tapestry needle
Accessories
Stitch holders
1 small snap
Elastic thread

notes

1 Use 2 plys of yarn held tog throughout.
2 Back and front are worked in one piece from the back to the front.
3 For sewing seams, use only one ply of yarn.

gauge

6 sts and 9 rows to 1" over St st using size 3 (3mm) needles and 2 plys of yarn held tog. FOR PROPER FIT, TAKE THE TIME TO CHECK YOUR GAUGE.

Scandinavian Ski Sets

The pink combination is textured with a nubby seed stitch and topped with a mixed-color yoke, the essence of Scandinavian ski sweaters. Matching pants and patterned hats complete the stunning sets.

FINISHING
Sew front, back and leg seams. Weave elastic thread through ribbing at waist and pull to gather.

hat

With B, cast on 28 sts. Work in k1, p1 rib for 4 rows. P 1 row for turning ridge. Cont in rib for 4 rows more. K 1 row.
Next row (WS) Change to A and work in St st for 7 rows.
Next (dec) row K2tog across—14 sts. P 1 row. Rep these 2 rows once more—7 sts.
Next (dec) row K2tog across, k1—4 sts.
Pull yarn through rem sts and pull tight to gather. Fasten off securely.
Embroidery
Straight-stitch one snowflake in center front of hat foll diagram. Sew back seam.
Decorative loops
With 2 plys of B and crochet hook, ch 7". Fasten off. Sew to top of hat making three loops.

pink sweater

SEED STITCH
Row 1 (RS) *K1, p1; rep from * to end.
Row 2 K the purl sts and p the knit sts.
Rep row 2 for seed st.

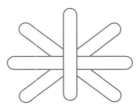

STRIPE PATTERN
Work in St st and stripes as foll: 3 rows A, 2 rows B, 2 rows A, 4 rows B.

With A, cast on 38 sts. Work in k1, p1 rib for 2 rows. Work in seed until piece measures 2½" from beg, end with a WS row.
Divide for Front and Backs
Work in St st and stripe pat, k8 (left back), bind off 2 sts, k18 (front), bind off 2 sts, k8 (right back).

RIGHT BACK
Next row (WS) P8, sl rem sts to holder. Cont even in stripe pat for 2 rows.
Next (dec) row K1, k2tog, work to end. P 1 row.
Rep last 2 rows 3 times more—4 sts. Sl to holder.

FRONT
P next 18 sts from holder. Cont in stripe pat for 2 rows.
Next (dec) row K1, k2tog work to last 3 sts, k2tog k1. P 1 row.
Rep last 2 rows 3 times more—10 sts. Sl to holder.

LEFT BACK
P last 8 sts from holder. Cont in stripe pat for 2 rows.
Next (dec) row K1, k2tog, work to end. P 1 row.
Rep last 2 rows 3 times more—4 sts. Sl to holder.

SLEEVES
With A, cast on 10 sts. Work in k1, p1 rib for 2 rows. Work in seed st, inc 1 st each side every 4th row 4 times—18 sts. Work even until piece measures 2½" from beg.
Raglan Shaping
Work in stripe pat, bind off 2 sts at

beg of next 2 rows.
Next (dec) row K1, k2tog, k to last 3 sts, k2tog, k1. P 1 row.
Rep last 2 rows 3 times more, then rep dec row once more—4 sts. Sl to holder.

FINISHING
Embroidery
With 1 ply of A, work zigzag stitch across first B-stripe, then work French knots in every other st around yoke.
Sew raglan seams, then sew sleeve seams.
Mock Turtleneck
With RS facing, sl sts from holders to needle—26 sts. K 1 row with A, then work in k1, p1 rib for 3 rows. Bind off loosely in rib.
Sew back seam, leaving top 1½" open at neck. Sew snap at turtleneck.

pink ski pants

(make 2 pieces)
Beg at waist, with A cast on 18 sts. Work in k1, p1 rib for 2 rows. Work in St st until piece measures 2" from beg.
Crotch Shaping
Cast on 2 sts at beg of next 2 rows—22 sts. Work even for 1½".
Leg Shaping
Dec 1 st at beg of next 2 rows, then every 6th row 3 times more—14 sts. Work even until piece measures 6½" from beg. Bind off.

FINISHING
Sew front, back and leg seams. Weave elastic thread through ribbing at waist and pull to gather.

hat

With A, cast on 28 sts. Work in k1, p1 rib for 4 rows. P 1 row for turning ridge. Cont in rib for 4 rows more. Work in St st for 3 rows.
Next row (WS) Change to B and work in St st for 2 rows. Then work 2 rows A.
Next (dec) row Change to B and k2tog across—14 sts. P 1 row. Rep these 2 rows once more—7 sts.
Next (dec) row K2tog across, k1—4 sts.
Pull yarn through rem sts and pull tight to gather. Fasten off securely.
Embroidery
Work zigzag stitch across first B-stripe, then work French knots in every third st across top of crown. Sew back seam.
Decorative Loops
With 2 plys of B and crochet hook, ch 7". Fasten off. Sew to top of hat making three loops.

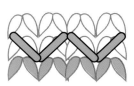

Reduce diagrams 50% for actual size.

materials

PINK SET
Yarn
Paternayan Persian by JCA (approx 8yd/7.4m) wool
7 skeins in #904 pink (A)
1 skein in #261 cream (B)
Needles
Size 3 (3mm) needles or size needed to obtain gauge,
Size B/1 (2mm) crochet hook
Tapestry needle
Accessories
Stitch holders
1 small snap
Elastic thread

notes

1 Use 2 plys of yarn held tog throughout.
2 Backs and front are worked in one piece to the underarm.
3 Use 1 ply of yarn to sew pieces tog.

gauge

6 sts and 9 rows to 1" over St st using size 3 (3mm) needles and 2 plys of yarn held tog
FOR PROPER FIT, TAKE THE TIME TO CHECK YOUR GAUGE.

Oversized Houndstooth Pullover

All checked out. Barbie® takes the bite out of winter with this oversized houndstooth check pullover. The black-and-white houndstooth pattern is never out of style, and a black collar, cuffs, and trim lend an extra-chic touch. The oversized shaping is designed to flatter any figure.

HOUNDSTOOTH CHECK PATTERN
(multiple of 4 sts)
Row 1 (RS) *K1 A, k1 B, k2 A; rep from * end.
Row 2 *P3 B, p1 A; rep from * to end.
Row 3 *K3 B, k1 A; rep from * to end.
Row 4 *P1 A, p1 B, p2 A; rep from * end.
Rep rows 1-4 for houndstooth check pat.

pullover

BACK
With A, cast on 42 sts. Work in k1, p1 rib for 2 rows. K 1 row A.
Beg Houndstooth Pat
K1 A, work houndstooth check pat over next 40 sts, k1 A. Cont as established, keeping the first and last sts as k1 A selvage st, until piece measures 3½" from beg, end with pat row 4.
Neck Shaping
Change to A and k16, join another strand of A and bind off center 10 sts, k16. Working both sides at once, work in k1, p1 rib for 3 rows. Place sts on holder.

FRONT
Work as for back.
Join shoulder seams tog using 3-needle bind-off.

SLEEVES
Place marker 1" down from shoulders on front and back. With A, pick up and k 22 sts between markers. Work in k1, p1 rib for 2 rows. P 1 row.
Beg Houndstooth Pat
K1 A, work houndstooth check pat over next 20 sts, k1 A. Cont as established, dec 1 st each side every 4th row 6 times—10 sts, end with row 4.
Next row (RS) With A, k 1 row. Work in k1, p1 rib for 3 rows. Bind off.

FINISHING
Sew side and sleeve seams.
Turtleneck
With A, cast on 44 sts. Work in k1, p1, rib for 1½". Bind off.
Sew back seam. Sew around neck. Fold down in half.

Color Key
■ Black A
○ White B

4-st rep

Yarn
Richesse Et Soie by K1C2, LLC (approx 145yds/132m) cashmere/silk
1 ball each in #9900 black (A) and #9100 white (B)
Needles
Size 1 (2.25mm) needles or size needed to obtain gauge
Accessories
Stitch holders

gauge

10 sts and 11 rows to 1" over houndstooth check pat using size 1 (2.25mm) needles.
FOR PROPER FIT, TAKE THE TIME TO CHECK YOUR GAUGE.

Ice Skating Outfits

Nice on ice.
The weather outside is frightful, but these skating outfits are most delightful. The green top features raglan sleeves, turtlenecks, and stockinette stitch, The red and white striped pattern of one and the embroidered "holly" pattern of the other make them the hottest things on ice.

green pullover

With A cast on 36 sts. Work in k1, p1 rib for 1".
Next row (RS) Work in reverse St st (p on RS, k on WS) for 6 rows, end with a WS row.
Divide for Fronts and Back
Change to B and St st. K8 (left back), bind off 2 sts, k16 (front), bind off 2 sts, k8 (right back).

RIGHT BACK
P8, place rem sts on holders. K 1 row, p 1 row.
Next (dec) row (RS) K1, k2tog, work to end. P 1 row.
Rep last 2 rows 3 times more—4 sts. Sl to holder.

FRONT
P16 sts from holder. K 1 row, p 1 row.
Next (dec) row (RS) K1, k2tog, work to last 3 sts, k2tog, k1. P 1 row.
Rep last 2 rows 3 times more—8 sts. Sl to holder.

LEFT BACK
P8 sts from holder. K 1 row, p 1 row.
Next (dec) row (RS) Work to last 3 sts, k2tog, k1. P 1 row.
Rep last 2 rows 3 times more—4 sts. Sl to holder.

SLEEVE
With A cast on 10 sts. Work in k1, p1 rib for 4 rows.
Next row (RS) Work in reverse St st, inc 1 st each side every 4th row 4 times—18 sts. Work even until sleeve measures 2¾" from beg, end with a WS row.
Raglan Shaping
Change to B and St st. Bind off 2 sts at beg of next 2 rows.

Next (dec) row (RS) K1, k2tog, work to last 3 sts, k2tog, k1. P 1 row.
Rep these 2 rows 4 times more—4 sts. Sl to holder.

FINISHING
Sew raglan seams. Sew sleeve seams.
Turtleneck
With RS facing, sl sts from holders to needle—24 sts. With A, knit, inc 4 sts evenly spaced. Work in k1, p1 rib for 7 rows. Bind off loosely in rib. Fold turtleneck down in half and loosely tack in place with A. Sew back seam, leaving 1½" from top edge of turtleneck open. Sew snap at turtleneck.
Embroidery
(Refer to photo as guide) With A, sew a zigzag running stitch around entire yoke for leaves. With C, work a French knot in center of each V-leaf.

green skirt

With A, beg at waist and cast on 21 sts.
Row 1 (RS) *K1, p1; rep from *, end k1.
Row 2 *P1, k1; rep from *, end p1.
Row 3 *K1, p1, M1 p-st; rep from *, end k1—31 sts.
Row 4 and all WS rows P the purl sts and k the knit sts.
Row 5 *K1, p2, M1 p-st; rep from *, end k1—41 sts.
Row 7 *K1, p3, M1 p-st; rep from *, end k1—51 sts.
Row 9 *K1, p4, M1 p-st; rep from *, end k1—61 sts.
Row 11 *K1, p5, M1 p-st; rep from *, end k1—71 sts.
Rows 12 to 16 Rep row 4.
Change to B.
Rows 17, 18 and 19 Knit.
Bind off knitwise.

materials

GREEN SET
Yarn
Paternayan Persian by JCA (approx 8yd/7.4m) wool
5 skeins in #611 green (A)
2 skeins #260 white (B)
1 skein of #968 red (C)
Needles
Size 3 (3mm) needles or size needed to obtain gauge
Tapestry needle
Accessories
Stitch holders
2 small snaps

notes

GREEN SET
1 Use 2 plys of yarn held tog throughout.
2 Use 1 ply of yarn for embroidery and to sew pieces tog.

gauge

6 sts and 9 rows to 1" over St st using size 3 (3mm) needles and 2 plys of yarn held tog.
FOR PROPER FIT, TAKE THE TIME TO CHECK YOUR GAUGE.

Ice Skating Outfits

The swingy skirts are knit in a ruffle stitch that increases from the waist down, starting with a 1 x 1 rib and ending in a white edging. Matching stocking hats with tiny pompoms make these sets utterly cap-tivating.

FINISHING
Sew back seam, leaving 1" open at waist. Sew snap to waist.

green stocking cap

With A, cast on 30 sts. Work in k1, p1 rib for 4 rows.
Next (dec) row (RS) Change to B, k1, k2tog, k to last 3 sts, k2tog, k1. P 1 row.
Rep these 2 rows 3 times more—22 sts.
Next (dec) row (RS) Change to A, p1, p2tog, p to last 3 sts, k2tog, k1. K 1 row.
Rep these 2 rows 8 times more—4 sts, end with WS row.
Next row (RS) P1, p2tog p1—3 sts.
Next row (WS) SK2P. Fasten off.

FINISHING
Sew back seam. Using 2 plys of B, embroider 5 loops at top of hat for pompom.
Embroidery
Embroider zigzag leaves and French knots flowers as for pullover.

red pullover

STRIPE PATTERN
Work in St st and stripes as foll: *2 rows B and 2 rows A; rep from * (4 rows) for stripe pat.

With A cast on 36 sts. Work in k1, p1 rib for 1". Work in stripe pat for 4 rows.
Divide for Front and Backs
Next row (RS) K8 sts (left back), bind off 2 sts, k16 (front), bind off 2 sts, k8 (right back).

RIGHT BACK
Cont in stripe pat, p8, sl rem sts to holders. K 1 row, p 1 row.
Next (dec) row (RS) K1, k2tog, work to end. P 1 row.
Rep last 2 rows 3 times more—4 sts. Sl to holder.

FRONT
Cont in stripe pat, p next 16 sts from holder. K 1 row, p 1 row.
Next (dec) row (RS) K1, k2tog, k to last 3 sts, k2tog, k1. P 1 row.
Rep last 2 rows 3 times more—8 sts. Sl to holder.

LEFT BACK
Cont in stripe pat, purl last 8 sts from holder. K 1 row, p 1 row.
Next (dec) row (RS) Work to last 3 sts, k2tog, k1. P 1 row.
Rep last 2 rows 3 times more—4 sts. Sl to holder.

SLEEVE
With A, cast on 10 sts. Work in k1, p1 rib for 4 rows. Work in stripe pat, inc 1 st each side every 4th row 4 times—18 sts. Work even until piece measures 3" from beg.
Raglan Shaping
Cont stripe pat, bind off 2 sts at beg of next 2 rows—14 sts.
Next (dec) row (RS) K1, k2tog, k to last 3 sts, k2tog, k1. P 1 row.
Rep last 2 rows 4 times more—4 sts. Sl to holder.

FINISHING
Sew raglan seams, matching stripes. Sew sleeve seams.

Turtleneck

With RS facing sl sts from holders to needle—24 sts. With A, k across, inc 4 sts evenly spaced. Work in k1, p1 rib for 7 rows. Bind off loosely in rib. Fold down turtleneck in half. Loosely tack in place with A.

Sew back seam, leaving 1½" open at turtleneck. Sew on snap to turtleneck.

red skirt

With A, beg at waist and cast on 21 sts.

Row 1 (RS) *K1, p1; rep from *, end k1.

Row 2 *P1, k1; rep from *, end p1.

Row 3 *K1, p1, M1 p-st; rep from *, end k1—31 sts.

Row 4 and all WS rows P the purl sts and k the knit sts.

Row 5 *K1, p2, M1 p-st; rep from *, end k1—41 sts.

Row 7 *K1, p3, M1 p-st; rep from *, end k1—51 sts.

Row 9 *K1, p4, M1 p-st; rep from *, end k1—61 sts.

Row 11 *K1, p5, M1 p-st; rep from *, end k1—71 sts.

Rows 12 to 16 Rep row 4.

Change to B

Rows 17, 18 and 19 Knit.

Bind off knitwise.

FINISHING

Sew back seam, leaving 1" open at waist. Sew snap to waist.

red stocking cap

With A, cast on 30 sts. Work in k1, p1 rib for 4 rows.

Next (dec) row (RS) Change to stripe pat, k1, k2tog, k to last 3 sts, k2tog, k1. P 1 row. Rep these 2 rows 12 times more—4 sts.

Next row (RS) K1, k2tog k1—3 sts.

Next row SK2P. Fasten off.

FINISHING

Sew back seam. With 2 plys of A, make 5 loops at top of hat for pompom.

materials

RED SET

Yarn

Paternayan Persian by JCA (approx 8yd/7.4m) wool
5 skeins in #968 red (A)
2 skeins in #260 white (B)

Needles

Size 3 (3mm) needles or size needed to obtain gauge
Tapestry needle

Accessories

Stitch holders
2 small metal snaps

notes

RED SET

1 Use 2 plys of yarn held tog throughout.

2 Use 1 ply of yarn for embroidery and to sew pieces tog.

3 Back and front are worked in one piece to the underarm.

gauge

6 sts and 9 rows to 1" over St st using size 3 (3mm) needles and 2 plys of yarn held tog. FOR PROPER FIT, TAKE THE TIME TO CHECK YOUR GAUGE.

Timely Twin Sets

Double the pleasure, double the fun. A neat twin set is the staple of the well-dressed woman's wardrobe, and this one is no exception. The cardigan and shell, both knit in stockinette, are perfect for a novice knitter's first sweater project. The simple shell, edged in ribbed trim, teaches basic armhole and neck shaping by decreasing, while the cardigan features sleeve increasing, a front band, and a collar—made the same way as a full-sized sweater.

cardigan

BACK
Cast on 27 sts. Work in k1, p1 rib for 2 rows. Work in St st until piece measures 2" from beg.

Armhole Shaping
Bind off 2 sts at beg of next 2 rows, then dec 1 st each side every other row twice—19 sts. Work even in St st until piece measures 3¼" from beg. Bind off.

LEFT FRONT
Cast on 15 sts. Work as for back, working armhole shaping at beg of RS rows only, until piece measures 3" from beg, end with a RS row.

Neck Shaping
Bind off 3 at neck edge sts once, then 1 st once—7 sts. Work even until piece measures same length as back. Bind off.

RIGHT FRONT
Work to correspond to left front, reversing all shaping.

SLEEVES
Cast on 14 sts. Work in k1, p1 rib for 2 rows. Work in St st, inc 1 st each side every 6th row twice—18 sts. Work even until piece measures 2½" from beg.

Cap Shaping
Bind off 2 sts at beg of next 2 rows, then dec 1 st each side every other row twice—10 sts. Work 2 rows even. Bind off 1 st at beg of next 4 rows. Bind off rem 6 sts.

FINISHING
Sew shoulder seams. Set in sleeves. Sew side and sleeve seams.

Front Bands
With RS facing, pick up 29 sts along left front. Work in k1, p1 rib for 1 row. Bind off in rib. Rep for right front.

Collar
With RS facing, pick up 29 sts evenly around neck. Work in k1, p1 rib for 1". Bind off in rib.
Sew buttons evenly spaced along left front band.

shell

BACK
With smaller needles, cast on 23 sts. Work in k1, p1 rib for 4 rows. Change to larger needles. Work in St st until piece measures 1½" from beg.

Armhole Shaping
Bind off 2 sts at beg of next 2 rows, then 1 st at beg of next 2 rows—17 sts. Work even until piece measures 2" from beg.

Neck Opening
Next row (RS) K9, join yarn, k8. Working each side separately, cont in St st until piece measures 3" from beg. Bind off.

FRONT
Work as for back until piece measures 2¼" from beg.

Neck Shaping
Next row (RS) K6 sts, join yarn and bind off 5 sts, work to end. Working each side separately, bind off 1 st at each neck edge once—5 sts. Work even until piece measures same length as back. Bind off.

FINISHING
Sew shoulder seams.

Neckband
With RS facing and smaller needles, pick up and k 33 sts evenly around neck. Work in k1, p1 rib for 1 row. Bind off in rib.

Armhole Bands
With RS facing and smaller needles, pick up and k 30 sts evenly around armhole. Work in k1, p1 rib for 1 row. Bind off in rib.
Sew side and armhole band seams. Sew snap to back neckband.

CARDIGAN

Yarn
True 4 Ply Botany by Rowan, 1¾oz/50g (approx 187yds/170mm) wool
1 skein in #573 lime

Needles
Size 1 (2.25mm) needles or size needed to obtain gauge

Accessories
Five ¼" yellow buttons

SHELL

Yarn
Paternayan Persian by JCA (approx 8yd/7.4m) wool
2 skeins in #333 lilac
OR
True 4 Ply Botany by Rowan, 1¾oz/50g (approx 187yds/170mm) wool
1 skein in #573 lime

Needles
Sizes 0 and 1 (2 and 2.25mm) needles or size needed to obtain gauge

Accessories
1 small snap

note
If using Paternayan Persian Yarn, use 1 ply only.

gauges

CARDIGAN
8 sts and 11 rows to 1" over St st using size 1 (2.25mm) needles and True 4 Ply Botany.

SHELL
8 sts and 11 rows to 1" over St st using size 1 (2.25mm) needles and True 4 Ply Botany OR 1 ply of Paternayan Persian Yarn.
FOR PROPER FIT, TAKE THE TIME TO CHECK YOUR GAUGES.

Tube Dress Bridal Party

A bouquet of bridal beauty. The bride and her bridesmaids make beautiful wedding belles in these simple but splendid gowns. Each dress—even the bride's—is knit in a tube style that requires no shaping. Knit as a flat stockinette piece, each dress is simply seamed up the back to form a clingy tube. The skirts and veil are made of tulle and sewn by hand, with appliqués stitched to the extra-special bridal gown.

dress

Beg at top of dress and cast on 32 sts. K 2 rows.
Next row (RS) Purl.
Cont in St st for 8". Bind off.
Sew back seam, leaving 1" open at top. Sew snap to upper edge.

skirt

WAIST BAND
Cast on 32 sts. Bind off.
Gather net along long edge and sew to band. Sew snap to band. For bridesmaid dress, sew rose on center front of band. For bride's dress, sew roses to lower edge of skirt spaced 2" apart. Sew a second set of roses 1" above first row, spaced evenly in between.

veil

VEIL BAND
Cast on 30 sts. Bind off. Sew band tog to form loop.
Fold down ½" of long side of net and gather to 1½". Sew band at fold of veil. Sew a rose to the band on each side of veil.

headpiece

HEADPIECE BAND
Cast on 10 sts. Bind off.
Gather long edge of net and sew to band.

bouquet

Gather net along long edge and tape around roses using floral tape. Sew ribbon under net. Use photo for guide.

Barbie Maid of Honor dress is worked same as bridesmaid dress using #1010 pink Metalica and pink netting.

BRIDE'S DRESS
Yarn
Metalica by Berroco, Inc., ⁷⁄₈oz/25g (approx 85yd/78m) rayon/metallic
1 skein of #1011 white
Accessories
White netting skirt: 40" x 6¼", veil: 20" x 7", bouquet: 1" x 20"
3 packages of opal roses from Offray Ribbon Boutique accessories, 2 small snaps. For bouquet: 2 dozen small white roses, three 2½" lengths of ⅛" white ribbon, small amount of floral tape

BRIDESMAID DRESS
Yarn
Metalica by Berroco, Inc., ⁷⁄₈oz/25g (approx 85yd/78m) rayon/metallic
1 skein of #1010 hollywood pink, #1008 sapphire, #1009 tournaline
Accessories
Rainbow netting; skirt: 40" x 6¼", headpiece: 15" x 2", bouquet: 1" x 20"
1 package of 4 different colored roses for bouquet and one package multi-colored roses from Offray Ribbon Boutique accessories, 2 small snaps, small amount of floral tape, three 2½" lengths of ⅛" ribbon (for bouquet)

NEEDLES FOR ALL DRESSES
Size 2 (2.5mm) needles or size to obtain gauge

gauge

7 sts and 10 rows to 1" over St st using size 2 (2.5mm) needles.
FOR PROPER FIT, TAKE THE TIME TO CHECK YOUR GAUGE.

Shimmering Evening Dresses

Ever the diva. Based on the famous "Solo in the Spotlight®" dress from 1960, this shapely black number is simply divine. A spray of tulle and a rosebud at the lower edge give it the magic touch. This simple gold evening gown becomes transformed in a glimmering yarn, delicate spaghetti straps, and a cluster of gilt roses. Add a tulle wrap with a haze of gold, and watch Barbie® step out into an enchanting evening.

black dress

Beg at top of dress and cast on 32 sts. K 2 rows.
Next row (RS) Purl. Work in St st for 6". Bind off.

FINISHING
Sew back seam, leaving open 1" at top. Sew snap to upper edge.

black skirt

Gather long edge of net and sew to bound off edge of dress. Sew rose at lower left edge of dress above skirt.

BLACK DRESS
Yarn
Metalica by Berroco, ⅞oz/25g
(approx 85yds/78m)
rayon/metallic
1 skein in #1012 black
Needles
Size 2 (2.5mm) needles or
size to needed to obtain
gauge
Accessories
Black netting 40" x 3"
Sewing thread
2 small snaps
1 pink ribbon rose by Offray
GOLD DRESS
Yarn
Metalica by Berroco, ⅞oz/25g
(approx 85yds/78m)
rayon/metallic
1 skein in #1001 gold
Needles
Size 2 (2.5mm) or size needed
to obtain gauge
Accessories
5 gold roses from Offray
Ribbon
21" x 6" netting in white with
gold flecks

gold dress

Beg at top of dress and cast on
32 sts. K 2 rows.
Next row (RS) Purl. Work in St
st for 8". Bind off.

FINISHING
Sew back seam, leaving open 1"
at top. Sew snap to upper edge.
Straps
(make 2)
Cast on 20 sts. Bind off.
Sew one strap to each side. Sew
5 roses on one strap.

gauge

7 sts and 10 rows to 1" over
St st using size 2 (2.5mm)
needles.
FOR PROPER FIT, TAKE THE
TIME TO CHECK YOUR GAUGE.

Elegant Camel Wrap

Park Avenue.
Every woman deserves a
touch of luxury, and for
Barbie, this is it. No
matter where she goes,
she oozes sophistication
in this elegant, all–
purpose wrap, knit in
camel–colored cashmere
with more than a touch
of silk. The stockinette–
stitched wrap is finished
off with a classy seed–
stitch border and
flowing fringe.

Yarn
Richesse et Soie by Knit One Crochet Too .88oz/25g (approx 145yd/132m) cashmere/silk
1 ball in #9448 camel
Needles
Size 1 (2.25) needles or size needed to obtain gauge
Size B/1 (2mm) crochet hook

SEED STITCH

Row 1 *K1, p1; rep from * to end.
Row 2 K the purl sts and p the knit sts.
Rep row 2 for seed st.

stole

BACK

Cast on 63 sts. Work 3 rows in seed st.
Next row (WS) Work 3 sts in seed st, p to last 3 sts, work 3 sts in seed st.
Cont in St st, keeping the first and last 3 sts in seed st until piece measures 4" from beg, end with a WS row.
Next row (RS) Work 27 sts, work in k1, p1 rib across center 9 sts, work to end. Rep this row once more.
Next row (RS) Work 27 sts, k1, p1, k1, bind off center 3 sts for neck, k1, p1, k1, work to end.

FRONTS

Work 27 sts, k1, p1, k1—30 sts for left front, join new yarn, k1, p1, k1, work to end—30 sts for right front. Working both sides at once, cont in St st, keeping the first and last 3 sts each side in seed st until fronts measure 4" from neck, end with a WS row. Work 3 rows seed st.

FRINGE

Cut 2½" lengths of yarn. With crochet hook and 2 lengths held tog, work fringe in every other st, along fronts and back. Trim fringe evenly.

gauge

9 sts and 12 rows to 1" over St st using size 1 (2.25mm) needles.
FOR PROPER FIT, TAKE THE TIME TO CHECK YOUR GAUGE.

Snowflake Pullover

Snow man.
Ken® is sure to win a gold medal in this handsome pullover. The bold snowflake, set off crisply against a crimson background, can be worked in intarsia or duplicate stitch. The neckband, cuffs, and lower edge are all knit in snow-white ribbing, which is repeated in his coordinating cap.

pullover

BACK

With B, cast on 26 sts. Work in k
p1 rib for 2 rows.
Change to A and work in St st u
piece measures 2½" from beg.

Armhole Shaping

Bind off 3 sts at the beg of next
rows—20 sts. Work even for 2 ro

Neck Opening

Next row (RS) K10, join yarn, k1
Working both sides at once, wor
even until piece measures 4½" fr
beg. Bind off.

Yarn
Paternayan Persian by JCA
(approx 8yd/7.4m) wool
5 skeins in #968 red (A)
1 skein in #263 white (B)
Needles
Size 2 (2.5mm) needles or
size needed to obtain gauge

FRONT

With B, cast on 25 sts. Work in k1,
p1 rib for 2 rows.
Change to A and work in St st until
piece measures 1¼" from beg.

Beg Chart
K6 A, work 13 sts of snowflake
chart, k6 A. Cont as established
through row 12.

Armhole Shaping
Cont as established and bind off 3
sts at the beg of next 2 rows—19
sts. Work even through chart row
17. Then cont in St st and A only
until armhole measures 1¼", end
with a WS row.

Neck Shaping
Next row (RS) K7, join yarn and
bind off center 5 sts, work to end.
Working both sides at once, dec 1 st
at neck edge once more. Work even
until same length as back to
shoulder. Bind off.

SLEEVES

With B, cast on 14 sts. Work in k1,
p1 rib for 2 rows. Change to A and
work in St st, inc 1 st each side
every 4th row 3 times—20 sts. Work
even until piece measures 3½" from
beg. Bind off.

FINISHING

Sew shoulder seams.

Neck Band
With RS facing and B, pick up and k
25 sts evenly around neck edge.
Work in k1, p1 rib for 2 rows.
Bind off.
Set in sleeves. Sew side and
sleeve seams.

hat

With B, cast on 27 sts. Work in k1,
p1 rib for 4 rows. K 1 row.
Next row (WS) P1 A, *p1 B, p1 A;
rep from * to end.
Next row K1 A, *k1 B, k1 A; rep
from * to end.
Rep these 2 rows once more.
Change to A and work in St st for 3
rows.
Next (dec) row (RS) K1, [k2tog]
across—14 sts. P 1 row.
Next (dec) row (RS) K2tog across—
7 sts. Draw yarn through rem sts
and gather tightly. Fasten off. Sew
back seam.

Color Key
■ Red A
○ White B

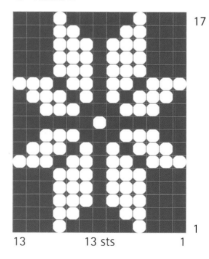

note

Use 2 plys of yarn held tog
throughout.

gauge

6 sts and 9 rows to 1" over St
st using size 2 (2.5mm)
needles and 2 plys of yarn
held tog.
FOR PROPER FIT, TAKE THE
TIME TO CHECK YOUR GAUGE.

Wrapped Jacket

Cover girl.
Barbie® keeps time with the city beat in this sensuous shawl–collared jacket, knit with one strand each of silk and cashmere and silk and mohair. The plush shawl collar, shaped with short rows, folds back to reveal the knit one, purl one rib underside, which adds a fleecy texture to the sleek stockinette-stitch body. Patch pockets are knit separately and then sewn on, and a tiny knit tie cinches the waist and completes the jacket.

cardigan

BACK
Cast on 23 sts. Work in k1, p1 rib for 3 rows. Work in St st until piece measures 4" from beg.

Armhole Shaping
Bind off 3 sts at beg of next 2 rows—17 sts. Cont in St st until armhole measures 1". Bind off.

LEFT FRONT
Cast on 15 sts. Work as for back until piece measures 3" from beg.

Neck Shaping
Next row (RS) K to last 3 sts, ssk, k1. Cont to dec 1 st at neck edge every 6th row 4 times more, AT THE SAME TIME, when piece measures 4" from beg, work armhole shaping at beg of RS rows as for back—7 sts. Bind off.

RIGHT FRONT
Work to correspond to left front, reversing all shaping and working neck shaping as foll: K1, k2tog, work to end.

SLEEVES
Sew shoulder seams.
Pick up and k 18 sts along armhole. Work in St st, dec 1 st each side every 6th rows 3 times—12 sts. Work in k1, p1 rib for 2 rows. Bind off.

FINISHING
Sew side and sleeve seams.

Shawl Collar
With RS facing, beg at neck shaping on right front, pick up and k 22 sts along right front, 7 sts along back, 22 sts along left front—51 sts.

Short Row Shaping
Next row (RS) Rib to last 2 sts, turn.
Next row (WS) Rib to last 2 sts, turn.
Next row (RS) Rib to last 4 sts, turn.
Next row Rib to last 4 sts, turn.
Cont as established, working 2 sts less each time, 10 times more. Work 1 row even. Bind off in rib.

POCKETS
(make 2)
Cast on 7 sts. Work in St st for ¾". Work in k1, p1 rib for 2 rows. Bind off in rib. Sew pockets to fronts.

BELT
Cast on 63 sts. Bind off 63 sts.

materials

Yarn
Douceur et Soie by Knit One, Crochet Too, .88oz/25g (approx 225yds/205m) mohair/silk
1 ball in #840 in light yellow (A)
Richesse et Soie, .88oz/25g (approx 145yds/132m) cashmere/silk
1 ball in #940 light yellow (B)

Needles
Size 2 (2.5mm) needles or size needed to obtain gauge

note
Work with 1 strand each of A and B held tog throughout.

gauge
7 sts and 9 rows to 1" over St st using size 2 (2.5mm) needles and 1 strand A and B held tog.
FOR PROPER FIT, TAKE THE TIME TO CHECK YOUR GAUGE.

Alpaca Cardigan

Chien charm.
A dog may be man's best friend, but this classy, cozy cardigan can't be far behind. Who wouldn't enjoy the luxury of alpaca in this shawl-collared cardigan, complete with roomy patch pockets for puppy treats? The body is knit in stockinette stitch with subtle stripes across the chest and arms. The shawl collar is worked in 1 x 1 rib stitch with short rows for shaping. All that's needed are a pipe and slippers to complete this fetching look.

cardigan

BACK

With smaller needles and A, cast on 28 sts. Work in k1, p1 rib for 2 rows. Change to larger needles, and work in St st until piece measures 2" from beg. Cont in St st and work 2 rows B, 2 rows A, work 2 rows B.

Armhole Shaping

Cont with A, bind off 2 sts at beg of next 2 rows, dec 1 st each side every other row twice—20 sts. Work even until piece measures 4" from beg. Bind off.

LEFT FRONT

With smaller needles and A, cast on 13 sts. Work as for back, working armhole shaping at beg of RS rows only, and when piece measures 3", beg neck shaping.

Neck Shaping

Next row (RS) Work to last 3 sts, ssk, k1. Cont to dec 1 st at neck edge every 4th row once more—7 sts. Work even until piece measures 4" from beg. Bind off.

RIGHT FRONT

Work to correspond to left front, reversing all shaping and working neck shaping at beg of RS rows as foll: k1, k2tog, work to end.

SLEEVES

With smaller needles, cast on 16 sts. Work in k1, p1 rib for 2 rows. Change to larger needles. Work in St st, inc 1 st each side every 4th row 3 times, AT SAME TIME, when piece measures 2" from beg, work stripe

pat as foll: 2 rows B, 2 rows A, 2 rows B—22 sts. Work even until piece measures 3" from beg.

Cap Shaping

Bind off 2 sts at beg of next 2 rows.
Next row K1, k2tog, work to last 3 sts, ssk, k1. P 1 row. Rep last 2 rows 3 times more. Bind off rem 10 sts.

POCKETS

With smaller needles cast on 7 sts. Work in St st for ½". Work in k1, p1 rib for 2 rows. Bind off.

FINISHING

Sew shoulder seams.

Front Bands and Collar

With RS facing and smaller needles, pick up and k 29 sts along right front edge to first neck dec, pm, pick up 31 sts around back neck to first neck dec of left front, pm, 29 sts along left front edge—89 sts. Work 3 rows in k1, p1 rib.

Beg Short Row Shaping

Next row (RS) Rib to 2nd marker, turn.
Next row (WS) Rib to marker, turn.
Next row (RS) Rib to last 2 sts before marker, turn.
Next row Rib to last 2 sts before marker, turn. Cont as established, working 2 sts less each time 9 times more, turn and rib to end. Bind off in rib.
Set in sleeves. Sew side and sleeve seams. Sew on buttons evenly spaced along left band. Sew pockets to fronts.

materials

Yarn

Alpaca 18 by Rainbow Gallery (approx 12yd/11m) alpaca
5 cards in #AL54 tan (A)
1 card in #AL53 cream (B)

Needles

Sizes 1 and 2 (2.25 and 2.5mm) needles or size needed to obtain gauge

Accessories

Stitch holders
5 buttons by JHB #47375 tan
Barbie button

gauge

8 sts and 10 rows to 1" over St st using size 2 (2.5mm) needles.
FOR PROPER FIT, TAKE THE TIME TO CHECK YOUR GAUGE.

Fur Collar Cashmere

Winter wonderland. Barbie® is an angelic vision in a fantasy of fur and cashmere. Her sumptuous baby blue cardigan is knit of pure cashmere in a stockinette stitch that enhances its smooth, silky texture, and is tipped with the luxurious fluff of Angora in the collar and cuffs. An Angora headband halo lends a heavenly touch. Tiny pearl buttons provide the perfect closure.

cardigan

BACK
With smaller needles and A, cast on 25 sts. Work in k1, p1 rib for ½". Change to larger needles.
Next row (RS) Work in St st, inc 1 st each side—27 sts. Cont in St st until piece measures 1¾" from beg.
Armhole Shaping
Bind off 2 sts at beg of next 2 rows, then 1 st at beg of next 2 rows—21 sts. Work even until piece measures 3" from beg. Bind off.

LEFT FRONT
With smaller needles and A, cast on 14 sts. Work in k1, p1 rib for ½". Change to larger needles.
Next row (RS) K10, p1, k1 ,p1, k1.
Next row P1, k1, p1, k1, p10. Rep last 2 rows until piece measures 1¾" from beg.
Armhole Shaping
Work as for back working armhole shaping at beg of RS rows only—11 sts. Work even until piece measures 2½" from beg.
Neck Shaping
Bind off 4 sts at neck edge. Then dec 1 st at neck once—6 sts. Work even until same length as back. Bind off.

RIGHT FRONT
Work to correspond to left front, reversing all shaping.

SLEEVES
With larger needles and B, cast on 13 sts. K 6 rows.
Next row (RS) With A, work in St st, inc 1 st each side, then every 6th row 3 times more—21 sts.
Cap Shaping
Bind off 2 sts at beg of next 2 rows, then dec 1 st each side every other row 6 times—5 sts. Bind off.

FINISHING
Sew shoulder seams.
Collar
With RS facing, larger needles and B, pick up and k 19 sts evenly around neck. Work in garter st for 1". Bind off.
Set in sleeves. Sew side and sleeve seams.
Sew buttons evenly along right front band. Sew snaps at neck and lower edge.

headband

With larger needles and B, cast on 30 sts. K 6 rows. Bind off. Sew snap to each end.

Yarn
Cashmere by Rainbow Gallery (each card approx 9yds/8.2m) cashmere
6 cards in #8 baby blue (A)
Angora by Rainbow Gallery (each card approx 7yds/6.4m) angora
1 card in #1 white (B)
Needles
Sizes 0 and 1 (2 and 2.25mm) needles or size to obtain gauge
Accessories
6 JHB white pearl buttons, #25003
3 sets of snaps

gauge

9 sts and 12 rows to 1" over St st using size 1 (2.25mm) needles and cashmere.
FOR PROPER FIT, TAKE THE TIME TO CHECK YOUR GAUGE.

Loop Ensemble

My Fair Lady.
In the markets of London
or on the streets of New
York, Barbie® doll cuts a
striking figure in this
lovely, loopy ensemble.
The neat, fitted suit is
worked in stockinette
stitch, then artfully
edged with a contrasting
loop-stitch fringe on
the jacket and hat. The
sheath dress underneath
features a striped bodice
and a dainty garter-
stitch hem. Embroidered
flowers bloom on the
jacket's sleeves and front.

My Fair Lady is a trademark of CBS Worldwide, Inc., used with permission.

LOOP STITCH
Row 1 (WS) Purl.
Row 2 Make loop K1, *insert RH needle as to k into next st, wrap yarn over needle and one finger of left hand 3 times (3 loops on needle), then once more to k1 through all loops; then insert LH needle into the front of the loop on the RH needle and k tbl; rep from * to last st, k1. Bind off.

dress

With B cast on 44 sts. K 2 rows. Change to A and work in St st until piece measures 1½" from beg.
Next (dec) row (RS) K10, k2tog, k20, k2tog, k10—42 sts. Work in St st for 1".
Next (dec) row (RS) K9, k2tog, k20, k2tog, k9—40 sts. Work in St st for 1".

Reduce diagrams 50% for actual size

Next (dec) row (RS) K8, k2tog, k20, k2tog, k8—38 sts. Work even in St st until piece measures 4½" from beg.
Beg Stripe Pat
Work in St st and stripes as foll: 2 rows B, 2 rows A, 2 rows B, 4 rows A, 4 rows B, 2 rows A, 2 rows B, 2 rows A, 4 rows B, 4 rows A.
Next row (RS) With B only, k8 (left back), bind off 2 sts, k18 (front), bind off 2 sts, k8 (right back).

RIGHT BACK
Next row (WS) P8 and place rem sts on holder. Work even in St st for 1". Bind off.

FRONT
Attach B and work across next 18 sts from holder. Work even in St st for 1". Bind off.

LEFT BACK
Attach B and work as for right back.

FINISHING
Sew shoulder seams.
Neck Band
With RS facing and A, pick up 14 sts along neck edge. K 2 rows. Bind off. Sew back seam, leaving 1" open for neck. Sew snap at neck edge.

jacket

With A cast on 42 sts. Work in St st for 4".
Armhole Shaping
Next row (RS) K9 (right front), bind off 3 sts, k18 (back), bind off 3 sts, k9 (left front).

LEFT FRONT
P9, place rem sts on holder. Work 5 rows in St st.
Neck Shaping
Next row (WS) P2tog, work to end. Cont to dec 1 st at neck edge every other row twice more—6 sts. Work even until armhole measures 1". Bind off.

BACK
Attach A and work across next 18 sts from holder. Work in St st until armhole measures 1". Bind off

RIGHT FRONT
Work to correspond to left front, reversing shaping.

SLEEVES
With A cast on 11 sts. Work in St st, inc 1 st each side every 12th row twice—15 sts. Work even until piece measures 3¼" from beg. Bind off

FINISHING
Embroider lower edge of fronts and sleeves with B, using lazy daisy, stem and straight sts (see diagram). Sew shoulder seams. Sew sleeve seams. Set in sleeves.
Loop Stitch Edging
With RS facing and B, beg at lower right front edge and pick up 28 sts to center back neck. Work loop st over all sts. Bind off. Work left front to correspond. Sew loop st edgings tog at back neck.
Pick up 33 sts along lower edge. Work loop st over all sts. Bind off. Sew hook and eye to center front.

hat

With A, cast on 27 sts. Work St st for ¾".
Next (dec) row K1, [k2tog] across—14 sts. P 1 row.
Next (dec) row K1, [k2tog] across, end k1—8 sts. P 1 row.
Next (dec) row K2tog across—4 sts. Pass rem sts over first st and fasten off.
With B, pick up 26 sts around lower edge and work loop st. Bind off. Sew back seam.

Yarn
Frosting by Knit One Crochet Too, 1¾oz/50g (approx 190yds/174m) cotton/nylon 1 ball each in #565 evergreen (A) and #510 celadon (B)
Needles
Size 2 (2.5mm) needles or size needed to obtain gauge
Tapestry needle
Accessories
Stitch holders
Small hook and eye
Small snap

note
Back and front are worked in one piece to the underarm.

gauge
15 sts and 12 rows to 2" over St st using size 2 (2.5mm) needles.
FOR PROPER FIT, TAKE THE TIME TO CHECK YOUR GAUGE.

Teatime Tweed Suits

Ladies who lunch. Black and white blends in a cotton yarn to create a tweedy look in the peplum. The jacket is knit up from the bottom and shaped with decreases to create a peplum that enhances a tiny waist.

Yarn
JAWoll Cotton Superwash by
Lang/Berroco, Inc., 1½oz/45g
(approx 190yds/175m)
wool/cotton/nylon
1 ball in #8803 black/white
tweed
Needles
Size 2 (2.5mm) needles or
size needed to obtain gauge
Accessories
Stitch holders
3 JCA buttons #13056 in
black
3 small black snaps,
#2 Elastic Thread by Knit One
Crochet Two in white

black and white jacket

Cast on 50 sts. K 2 rows. Work in rev St st and inc 1 st each side every other row 3 times—56 sts.
Next row (RS) [K1, p1] twice k1, p2tog across to last 5 sts, k1, [p1, k1] twice—33 sts. Work in k1, p1 rib for 3 rows.
Next row (RS) [K1, p1] twice, p to last 3 sts, k1, p1, k1.
Next row (WS) P1, k1, p1, *k3, inc 1; rep from * to last 3 sts, p1, k1, p1—42 sts.
Cont as established, working the first and last 3 sts in rib, for 1" more.
Divide for Armholes
Next row (RS) Work 11 sts and place on holder (right front), bind off 2 sts, work 16 sts (back), bind off 2 sts, place rem 11 sts on holder (left front).

BACK
Cont in rev St st until armhole measures 1½". Bind off.

RIGHT FRONT
Next row (WS) K8, p1, k1, p1.
Next row K1 p1, k1, p2tog, p6. Rep last 2 rows 3 times more—7 sts. Work 4 rows even.
Next row (WS) Bind off 4 sts, rib 3 sts. Cont in rib on rem 3 sts for ½" more for neckband. Bind off.

LEFT FRONT
Work to correspond to right front, reversing all shaping.

SLEEVES
Cast on 12 sts. K 2 rows. Work in rev St st, inc 1 st each side every 10th row twice—16 sts. Work even until piece measures 2½" from beg.
Cap Shaping
Bind off 1 st at beg of next 10 rows. Bind off rem 6 sts.

FINISHING
Sew shoulder seams. Sew neckband seam and sew to back neck. Set in sleeves. Sew sleeve seams. Sew a snap at waist and at neck. Sew 3 buttons evenly spaced along left front between waist and neck. Run 2 rows of elastic through waist ribbing.

Back and front are worked in one piece to the underarm.

7 sts and 10 rows to 1" over St st using size 2 (2.5mm) needles.
FOR PROPER FIT, TAKE THE TIME TO CHECK YOUR GAUGE.

Teatime Tweed Suits

A variegated-color cotton is used for the herringbone suit to create a variety of patterns within the fabric. The tweed hat features the texture of reverse stockinette stitch, while the herringbone hat sports a rolled-edge look with stockinette.

skirt

Cast on 38 sts. K 2 rows. Work in St st for 3". Work in k1, p1 rib for 3 rows (for waistband). Bind off.

FINISHING
Sew back seam, leaving 1" open at waistband. Sew snap to waistband. Run elastic twice through waistband

black and white hat

Cast on 39 sts for brim. Work rev St st for 1", end with a WS row.
Next (dec) row (RS) *K2, k2tog; rep from *, end k3—30 sts. Cont in St st for 7 rows.
Next (dec) row (RS) K1, *k2tog, rep from *, end k1—16 sts.
Next (dec) row P2tog across—8 sts.
Next (dec) row K2tog across—4 sts.
Pass rem sts over first st. Fasten off. Sew back seam.

pink and grey jacket

Cast on 42 sts. K 2 rows.
Next row (WS) [P1, k1] twice, p to last 4 sts, [k1, p1] twice.
Next row (RS) [K1, p1] twice, p to last 4 sts, [p1, k1] twice.
Rep last 2 rows until piece measures 1½" from beg, end with a WS row.
Divide for Armholes
Next row (RS) Work 12 sts and place on holder (right front), bind off 2 sts, work 14 sts (back), bind off 2 sts, place rem 12 sts on holder (left front).

BACK
Cont in St st until piece measures 3" from beg. Bind off.

RIGHT FRONT
Next row (WS) P8, [k1, p1] twice. Cont as established until piece measures 2½" from beg.
Neck Shaping
Next row (RS) Bind off 4 sts in rib, work to end. Dec 1 st at neck edge on next RS row.
Work until same length as back. Bind off rem 7 sts.

LEFT FRONT
Next row (RS) Work to correspond to right front, reversing all shaping.

SLEEVES
Cast on 12 sts. K 2 rows. Work in St st, inc 1 st each side every 10th row twice—16 sts. Work even until piece measures 2½" from beg.
Cap Shaping
Bind off 1 st at beg of next 10 rows. Bind off rem 6 sts.

FINISHING
Sew shoulder seams. Set in sleeves. Sew sleeve seams. Sew on a snap at waist and neck. Sew 3 buttons evenly spaced along right front.
Collar
With WS facing, pick up and k 19 sts evenly spaced between front rib bands. Work in k1, p1 rib for 1". Bind off.
Fold front rib bands back and sew in place.

pink and grey hat

Cast on 39 sts for brim. Work St st for 1", end with a WS row.
Next (dec) row (RS) *K2, k2tog; rep from *, end k3—30 sts. Cont in St st for 7 rows.
Next (dec) row (RS) K1, *k2tog, rep from *, end k1—16 sts.
Next (dec) row P2tog across—8 sts.
Next (dec) row K2tog across—4 sts.
Pass rem sts over first st. Fasten off. Sew back seam.

skirt

Cast on 38 sts. K 2 rows. Work in St st for 3". Work in k1, p1 rib for 3 rows (for waistband). Bind off.

FINISHING
Sew back seam, leaving 1" open at waistband. Sew snap to waistband. Run elastic twice through waistband

Yarn
JAWoll Cotton Superwash by Lang/Berroco, Inc., 1½oz/45g (approx 190yds/175m) wool/cotton/nylon
1 ball in #8278 pink/grey multi

Needles
Size 2 (2.5mm) needles or size needed to obtain gauge

Accessories
Stitch holders
3 JCA buttons #47374 in pink
2 small snaps
#2 Elastic Thread by Knit One Crochet Two in white

note

Back and front are worked in one piece to the underarm.

gauge

7 sts and 10 rows to 1" over St st using size 2 (2.5mm) needles.
FOR PROPER FIT, TAKE THE TIME TO CHECK YOUR GAUGE.

"Fur"-Trimmed Zebra-Print Coat

Wild life.

What's black and white and red all over? The stylish woman who paints the town in this fabulous fur-trimmed zebra coat. She shows her stripes—knit in intarsia—in this stunning number worked in one piece from a chart and assembled with side and sleeve seams. Black Angora on the border, collar, and hat adds a touch of sophistication to this exotic look. As every wild thing knows, zebra stripes never go out of style.

coat

BACK
With smaller needles and A, cast on 30 sts. K 1 row. Change to larger needles.
Beg Zebra Chart
Work foll, chart through row 30.

SLEEVES
Cont to foll chart, cast on 5 sts at beg of next 6 rows—60 sts. Work even through row 42.

Neck Shaping
Work 25 sts, join new yarn and bind off center 10 sts, work to end. Working both sides at once, dec 1 st at each neck edge every other row twice—23 sts each side. Work through chart row 47.

FRONT
Cont to work both sides separately, and working chart rows 47 to 1, working neck incs instead of decs.

SLEEVES
Bind off 5 sts at beg of next 6 rows—15 sts.
Cont to foll chart through row 1. Bind off with A.

FINISHING
Sleeve Bands
With smaller needles and C, pick up and k 20 sts around sleeve edge. K 1 row. Bind off. Sew side and sleeve seams.

Front Fur Band
With RS facing, smaller needles and C, pick up and k 39 sts along right front edge. K 1 row. Bind off. Rep for left front.

Lower Fur Band
With RS facing, smaller needles and C, pick up and k 48 sts around lower edge, including front bands. K 1 row. Bind off.

Collar
With RS facing, smaller needles and C, pick up and k 28 sts around neck. Work in garter st for 1". Bind off. Sew snaps to front, 1 at neck edge, under collar and 1 at center.

hat

With larger needles and C, cast on 28 sts. Work in garter st for ³⁄₄".
Next row K2tog across—14 sts. K 3 rows.
Next row K2tog across—7 sts.
Next row K2tog across, end k1—4 sts. Pull yarn through rem sts. Fasten securely. Sew back seam.

Yarn
Perle Cotton #3 by DMC, 3g (approx 16yd/15m) cotton 3 skeins each in black (A) and white (B)
Angora by Rainbow Gallery (approx 7yd/6.4m) angora 2 cards in #18 black (C)
Needles
Sizes 1 and 2 (2.25 and 2.5mm) needles or size needed to obtain gauge
Accessories
1 small hook and eye
3 JHB #16051 black doll buttons

notes

1 Zebra Coat is worked in one piece from the back to the front.
2 When changing colors, twist yarns on WS to prevent holes. Carry unused color loosely across back of work.
3 Read chart from right to left on RS rows, from left to right on WS rows.

gauge

7 sts and 8 rows to 1" over St st using larger needles and Perle Cotton # 3.
FOR PROPER FIT, TAKE THE TIME TO CHECK YOUR GAUGE.

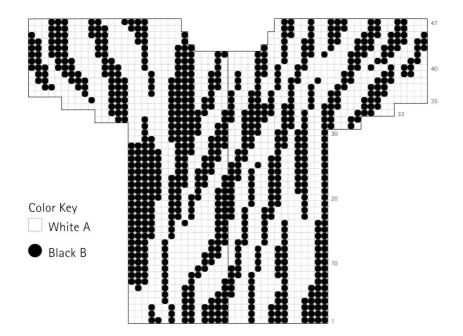

Color Key
☐ White A
● Black B

Beaded Tunic and Shawl Set

Uptown girl. Barbie® struts high style wrapped in this chic set, knit in soft silk. The close–fitting tunic is worked in a 1 x 1 rib stitch, which makes it hug Barbie® doll's curves in the most flattering way. Beads sewn into the ribbing at the neck and hem add a sophisticated touch. The essential silk wrap is knit in stockinette stitch and edged with the same beaded ribbing that adorns the tunic. A delicate fringe adds the finishing touch.

Yarn
Richesse Et Soie by Knit One,
Crochet Two, .88oz/25g,
(approx 145yd/132m)
cashmere/silk
1 ball in #9352 coral
Needles
Size 1 (2.25mm) needles or
size needed to obtain gauge
Small crochet hook
Accessories
Stitch holders
Glass beads in purple

sweater

BODY
Cast on 51 sts, Work in k1, p1 rib
for 3¼".
Divide for Armholes
Next row (RS) Rib 11 (left back),
join new yarn, bind off 3 sts, rib 23
(front), join new yarn, bind off 3 sts,
rib to end (right back).
Working all sides at once with
separate yarns, cont in rib until
piece measures 4" from beg.
Sl first 5 sts of left back to holder,
center 11 sts from front to holder
and last 5 sts from right back to a
holder. Then bind off shoulders using
a 3-needle bind-off.
Neck Shaping
With RS facing, rib 5 sts from left
back holder, pick up and p 1 st at
shoulder, work 11 sts from front
holder in rib, pick up and p 1 st at
shoulder, rib 5 sts from right back
holder—23 sts. Cont in k1, p1 rib for
½". Bind off loosely in rib.

FINISHING
Sew back seam.
Sew 2 rows of purple beads around
neck over purl sts. Sew 2 rows of
purple beads around lower edge over
purl sts.

shawl

Cast on 27 sts. Work in k1, p1 rib for
6 rows.
Next row (RS) Rib 4, k19, rib 4.
Work in St st, keeping the first and
last 4 sts in k1, p1 rib until piece
measures 13½" from beg.
Next row Work in k1, p1 rib across
all sts for 6 rows. Bind off.
Fringe
Cut 2" lengths. Attach to top and
bottom with small crochet hook (see
illustration). Trim even.
Sew 2 rows of beads over the purl
sts in the rib at top and lower edges.

note

Back and front are worked in
one piece to the underarm.

gauge

9 sts and 12 rows to 1" over
St st using size 1 (2.25mm)
needles.
FOR PROPER FIT, TAKE THE
TIME TO CHECK YOUR GAUGE.

Cold-Weather Accoutrements

Baby, it's cold outside! But Barbie® stays warm and fashionable in hat and scarf sets that provide the perfect accents for any outfit. Perhaps a rosy ribbed set peppered with pompoms or a garter-stitch set in stripes will do.

pompom scarf

Cast on 22 sts. Work in k2, p2 rib for 10". Bind off.
Sew 10 pompoms to each end.

hat

Cast on 46 sts. Work in k2, p2 rib for 1¾".
Next (dec) row (RS) *K2, p2tog; rep from *, end k2—35 sts.
Next row *P2tog, k1; rep from *, end p2tog—24 sts.
Next row K2tog across—12 sts.
Next row P2tog across—6 sts.
Next row Pass all sts over the first st and fasten off.
With crochet hook, ch 2". Sew center of ch to top of hat and attach a pompom to each end of ch.

welted stripe scarf

STRIPE PATTERN
With A, k 1 row, p 1 row; with B, work 6 rows garter st; with A, k 1 row, p 1 row; with C, work 6 rows garter st; with A, k 1 row, p 1 row; with D, work 6 rows garter st; with A, k 1 row, p 1 row; with E, work 6 rows garter st; with A, k 1 row, p 1 row; with F, work 6 rows garter st. Rep these 40 rows for stripe pat.

With A, cast on 6 sts. Work in stripe pat, working the 40-row rep 3 times, then with A, k 1 row, p 1 row. Piece measures approx 11½". Bind off.

hat

With A, cast on 10 sts. Work 32 rows of stripe pat. Bind off.
Sew cast-on edge to bound-off edge.
Gather one side edge for top of hat, leaving ends (do not weave in) for pompom at top. Trim ends evenly.

materials

POMPOM HAT AND SCARF
Yarn
Paternayan Persian by JCA (approx 8yd/7.4m) wool
2 skeins in #333 lilac
Needles
Size 1 (2.25mm) needles or size needed to obtain gauge
Small crochet hook
Accessories
1 Package Nicole 5mm pompoms
WELTED HAT AND SCARF
Yarn
Tapestry Wool by DMC (approx 8.7yds/8mm) wool
1 skein each in #7419 brown (A), #7423 tan (B), #7780 gold (C), #7411 beige (D), #7413 taupe (E), #7165 mauve (F)
Needles
Size 3 (3mm) needles or size needed to obtain gauge

note

POMPOM HAT AND SCARF
Use 1 ply of yarn throughout.

gauges

POMPOM HAT AND SCARF
15 sts and 11 rows to 1" over garter st using size 1 (2.25mm) needles and Paternayan Persian.
WELTED HAT AND SCARF
6 sts and 11 rows to 1" over stripe pat using size 3 (3mm) needles and Tapestry Wool.
FOR PROPER FIT, TAKE THE TIME TO CHECK THE GAUGES.

Cold-Weather Accoutrements

A ruffled hat and striped scarf might put her in the pink, or she may prefer a seed-stitch ensemble, which features a pull-through scarf and jaunty cap.

felted scarf

With A, cast on 11 sts. Work 2 rows in k1, p1 rib. Work in St st for 4 rows. Cont in St st and work 2 rows B, 2 rows A, 2 rows B, then work in A for 4". Work 2 rows B, 2 rows A, 2 rows B, 4 rows A, then work 2 rows in k1, p1 rib with A. Bind off.

hat

Beg at crown, with A cast on 5 sts.
Rows 1 (RS) *K1, M1; rep from * to end—9 sts.
Row 2 and all WS rows Purl.
Row 3 Rep row 1—17 sts.
Row 5 Rep row 1—33 sts.
Row 7 *K3, M1; rep from *, end k3—43 sts.
Next row With B, k 1 row, p 1 row.
Next row With A, k 1 row, p 1 row.
Next row With B, k 1 row, p 1 row. Work with A to end of piece. K 1 row. Work 1 row in k1, p1 rib.
Next row *K1, p1; rep from * to end.
Next row K1, *p1, M1 p-st, k1; repeat from * to end—64 sts. Work 1 row even.

Next row K1, *p2, M1 p-st, k1; rep from * to end—85 sts. Work 1 row even.
Next row K1, *p3, M1, k1; rep from * to end—106 sts. Work 1 row even.
Next row K1, *p4, M1, k1; rep from * to end—127 sts. Work 1 row even. Bind off. Sew back seam. Sew crown closed.

FELTING
Agitate hat and scarf in hot and cold water with laundry detergent until felted.

seed stitch scarf

SEED STITCH
(over an odd number of sts)
Row 1 *K1, p1; rep from *, end k1.
Rep row 1 for seed st.

Cast on 15 sts. Work in seed st
for 5".
Next row (RS) Work 7 sts, join new
yarn, bind off 1 st, work to end.
Work each side with separate
yarns for ³⁄₄".
Next row Work 7 sts, cast on 1 st,
work 7 sts. Cont in pat with single
strand for 2" more. Bind off in
seed st.

hat

Cast on 33 sts. Work in seed
st for 1".
Next (dec) row *K2tog, p2tog; rep
from *, end k1—17 sts.
Rep dec row—9 sts.
Cont in seed st on for ¹⁄₂" more. Bind
off in seed st. Sew back seam.

materials

FELTED HAT AND SCARF
Yarn
Paternayan Persian by JCA
(approx 8yd/7.4m) wool
1 skein each in #945 pink (A)
and #263 ecru (B)
Needles
Size 1 (2.25mm) needles or
size needed to obtain gauge
**SEED STITCH HAT AND
SCARF**
Yarn
Paternayan Persian by JCA
(approx 8yd/7.4m) wool
2 skeins of #004 multi
Needles
Size 0 (2mm) needles or size
needed to obtain gauge

note

**SEED STITCH HAT AND
SCARF**
Scarf and hat are worked
using one ply of yarn.

gauges

FELTED HAT AND SCARF
12 sts and 12 rows to 1" over
St st (after felting) using size
1 (2.25mm) needles.
**SEED STITCH HAT AND
SCARF**
7 sts and 7 rows to 1" over St
st using size 0 (2mm) needles
and 1 ply of yarn.
FOR PROPER FIT, TAKE THE
TIME TO CHECK THE GAUGES.

Cold-Weather Accoutrements

garter stitch scarf

Cast on 70 st. Work in garter st for 1¼".
Bind off.
Attach fringe to short edges.
(See illustration)
Fringe
Cut 2" lengths of yarn. With crochet
hook, attach single lengths every other
st around lower edge.
Trim evenly.

hat

Cast on 30 sts. Work in garter st
for 1¼".
Next (dec) row K2tog across—15 sts.
Next (dec) row K2tog across, end
k1—8 sts.
Next (dec) row K2tog across—4 sts
Pass the second, 3rd, and 4th sts over
the first st. Fasten off.
Sew back seam. Fold up lower edge
for brim.

Texture and color reign
in a rustic garter-stitch
set in variegated hues,
or a cabled set in two-
color stripes with tassels
to boot.

cable scarf

With A, cast on 22 sts. **Work in cable pat, working the 4-row rep 4 times. Change to B and work in cable pat, working the 4-row rep 4 times**. Rep between **'s twice, piece measures approx 9". Bind off.

CABLE PATTERN

Rows 1 and 3 (WS) K2, *p2, k2; rep from * to end.
Row 2 (RS) P2, *k2, p2; rep from * to end.
Row 4 P2, *knit the second st on LH needle, then knit the first st and slip both sts from needle tog, p2; rep from * to end.
Rep rows 1-4 for cable pat.

hat

With A, cast on 22 sts. Work in cable pat, working the 4-row rep 4 times. Change to B and work in cable pat, working the 4-row rep 4 times. Bind off. With WS tog, fold at color change and sew side seams. Make two 1" tassel with A and attach to each corner of hat.

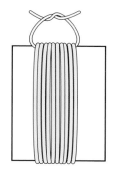

GARTER STITCH HAT AND SCARF
Yarn
JAWoll Cotton Superwash by Lang/Berroco, Inc., 1½oz/45g (approx 190yds/175m) wool/cotton/nylon
1 ball in #8280 multi
Needles
Size 2 (2.5mm) needles or size needed to obtain gauge
Accessories
Small crochet hook
CABLE HAT AND SCARF
Yarn
True 4 Ply Botany 4 Ply by Rowan 1¾oz/50g (approx 184yds/170m) wool
Small amount of each in #573 light green (A) and #575 dark green (B)
Needles
Size 1 (2.25mm) needles or size needed to obtain gauge

gauges

CABLE HAT AND SCARF
13 sts and 12 rows to 1" over cable pat using size 1 (2.25mm) needles and True 4 Ply.
GARTER STITCH HAT AND SCARF
7 sts and 15 rows to 1" over garter st using size 2 (2.5mm) needles and JAWoll Cotton Superwash.
FOR PROPER FIT, TAKE THE TIME TO CHECK THE GAUGES.

Funky "Fur" Coat

Fur–nomenal. Barbie® will be halting traffic wherever she goes in this funky, fluffy coat, knit in a novelty fur yarn in stoplight red. The coat is worked in simple garter stitch—the yarn's radiant personality takes over from there to create an effect that's simply dynamite. Top it with a matching fur hat, and she will turn heads all over the world.

coat

BACK
Cast on 20 sts. Work in garter st for 6".

SLEEVES
Cast on 12 sts at beg of next 2 rows—44 sts. Work even for 1½".
Shoulder and Neck Shaping
K20, join new yarn and bind off 4 sts (for neck), k20. Working both sides at once, inc 1 st at each neck edge every other row 3 times—23 sts each side.
Place marker at each neck edge. Work even until sleeve measures 3". Bind off 12 sts each side for each sleeve.
Work even on 11 sts each side until same length as back. Bind off.

COLLAR
Pick up 20 sts between markers. Work in garter st for 1¼". Bind off.

FINISHING
Sew side and sleeve seams. Sew hook and eye at waist.

hat

With A, cast on 10 sts. Work garter st for ¾".
Next (dec) row K2tog across—5 sts.
K 3 rows.
Next (dec) row K1, [k2tog] across—3 sts.
Pass rem sts over first st and fasten off. Sew back seam.

materials

Yarn
Furore by Lang/Berroco, Inc., 1¾oz/50g (approx 94yds/86m) nylon
1 ball in red multi
Needles
Size 3 (3mm) needles or size needed to obtain gauge
Accessories
Small hook and eye

note

Back and front are worked in one piece from the back to the front.

gauge

5 sts and 7 rows to 1" over garter st using size 3 (3mm) needles.
FOR PROPER FIT, TAKE THE TIME TO CHECK YOUR GAUGE.

Retro Vests and Caps

The sixties return—yet Barbie® remains as hip as ever in these groovy vests and skullcaps. A wispy novelty yarn adds a furry texture that makes these sets extra funky. Knit all in one piece in garter stitch, these easy-to-make vests can be adjusted in length—from tunic to cropped—to suit psychedelic tastes.

Yarn
Artic Rays Wispy Fringe by
Rainbow Gallery
(approximately 8yds/7.3m)
100% nylon
SHORT VEST
4 cards in #AR5 aqua (A)
AQUA HAT
1 card in #AR5 aqua (A)
LONG VEST
6 cards in #AR12 red (B)
RED HAT
1 card in #AR12 red (B)
Needles
Size 2 (2.5mm) needles or
size needed to obtain gauge

short vest

With A, cast on 23 sts for back.
Work in garter st for 3".
Next row (RS) K10 (right front), join
new yarn, bind off 3 sts (neck), work
to end (left front). Working both
sides at once, cont in garter st until
fronts are same length as back. Bind
off 10 sts each side.

FINISHING

Sew side seams leaving 1" open for
armholes.

long vest

With B, cast on 23 sts for back.
Work in garter st for 5½".
Next row (RS) K10 (right front), join
another strand of yarn, bind off 3
sts (neck), work to end (left front).
Working both sides at once, cont in
garter st until fronts are same
length as back. Bind off 10 sts
each side.

FINISHING

Sew side seams leaving 1" open for
amholes and 1" open at lower edge
for side slit.

hat

Cast on 28 sts. Work in garter st
for 1".
Next row K2tog across—14 sts.
Next row K2tog across—7 sts.
Pass 2nd, 3rd, 4th, 5th, and 6th st
over the first st and fasten off. Sew
back seam.

note

Back and front are worked in
one piece from the back to
the front.

gauge

8 sts and 12 rows to 1" over
St st using size 2 (2.5mm)
needles.
FOR PROPER FIT, TAKE THE
TIME TO CHECK YOUR GAUGE

Fuzzy Sleeveless Shell

Checks in the city. Every girl needs one of these—in every color. This chic sleeveless pullover perfectly tops everything, from wild checks and animal prints to a sleek leather mini. Worked in stockinette stitch, this top is ultra easy, and two strands of fuzzy novelty yarn make it purr with texture. Try using two different colors held together for a tweedy, totally unique look.

Yarn
Fuzzy Stuff by Rainbow
Gallery (approx 15yd/13.7m)
polyamide/viscose
3 cards in #209 lime

Needles
Size 3 (3mm) needles or size
needed to obtain the gauge

pullover

FRONT
With 2 strands held tog, cast on 15
sts. Work in k1, p1 rib for 3 rows.
Work in St st until piece measures
1½" from beg.

Sleeve Cap
Cast on 3 sts at beg of next 2
rows—21 sts.
Work even until piece measures 3"
from beg.
Next row (RS) K5, bind off center
11 sts (for neck), k5.

BACK
Next row (WS) P5, cast on 11 sts,
p5. Cont in St st for 1½".
Bind off 3 sts at beg of next 2
rows—15 sts. Work even until
piece measures same length as
front. Bind off.

FINISHING
Sew side and sleeve cap seams.

notes

1 Use 2 strands of yarn held
tog throughout.
2 Back and front are worked
in one piece from front to
the back.

gauge

6 sts and 8 rows to 1" using
size 3 (3mm) needles and 2
strands of yarn held tog.
FOR PROPER FIT, TAKE THE
TIME TO CHECK YOUR GAUGE.

Counterpane Poncho

Peace and love. Barbie® is always pretty in pink, particularly when it's worked into an intricate poncho that's a showcase of stitches. Each half of the poncho—four triangles stitched together—features a bounty of bobbles, ribs, eyelets, and more. The face-framing garter-stitch mock turtleneck is added after the poncho is assembled, and a flurry of fringes finishes the look.

MAKE BOBBLE
(MB)
[P1, k1] twice in same st—4 sts, then sl 2nd, 3rd, 4th, sts over first st.

poncho

(make 4 triangles)
Beg at neck and cast on 1 st. Work in counterpane pat and inc 1 st at end of every row 51 times as foll:
Row 1 (WS) Inc 1—2 sts.
Rows 2–12 K to last st, inc 1—13 sts.
Rows 13–16 Work in St st to last st, inc 1—17 sts.
Rows 17–21 Work in k2, p2 rib to last st, inc 1—22 sts.
Rows 22–24 Work in St st to last st, inc 1—25 sts.
Rows 25–31 Work in garter st to last st, inc 1—32 sts.
Rows 32 and 33 Work in St st to last st, inc 1—34 sts.
Row 34 (RS) K33, inc 1—35 sts.
Row 35 K2 [yo, k2tog] 16 times, inc 1—36 sts.
Row 36 K35, inc 1—37 sts.
Row 37 (WS) K36, inc 1—38 sts.
Row 38 P37, inc 1 p-st—39 sts.
Row 39 K2 [MB, k4] 7 times, MB, inc 1—40 sts.

Row 40 P39, inc 1 p-st—41 sts.
Row 41 K40, inc 1—42 sts.
Row 42 K41, inc 1—43 sts.
Row 43 K2 [yo, k2tog] 20 times, inc 1—44 sts.
Row 44 K43, inc 1—45 sts.
Rows 45 and 46 Work in St st to last st, inc 1—47 sts.
Rows 47–52 Work in garter st to last st, inc 1—52 sts.
Bind off.

FINISHING
Sew 2 triangles tog to form half of poncho. Sew halves tog, leaving 1" open on last seam for neck.
Neckband
Cast on 28 sts. Work in garter st for 1". Bind off.
Sew band loosely around neck, overlapping rem end. Sew snap on overlap. Sew beads at side edge.
Fringe
Cut 2" lengths of yarn. With crochet hook, attach single lengths every other st around lower edge.
Trim evenly.

Yarn
True 4 ply Botany by Rowan, 1¾oz/50g (approx 184yds/170m) wool
1 skein in #579 pink
Needles
Size 2 (2.5mm) needles or size needed to obtain gauge
Small crochet hook
Accessories
1 small snap
3 small pink beads (optional)

gauge

7 sts and 14 rows to 1" over garter st using size 2 (2.5mm) needles.
FOR PROPER FIT, TAKE THE TIME TO CHECK YOUR GAUGE.

Chunky-Knit Pullover

First impressions. When enjoying the still life, Barbie® reaches for the ultimate in cuddly comfort—a chunky, cropped pullover. This version is crafted in teal wool with a cozy turtleneck, picture-perfect for chilly days. The best designs are the most versatile, and this one is no exception: simply increase the length to create a tunic, dress, or gown. The sleek shaping is perfect for all four looks.

pullover

BACK

Cast on 13 sts. Work in k1, p1 rib for 2 rows. Work in St st until piece measures 2" from beg, end with a WS row.

Neck Shaping

Next row (RS) K4, bind off 5 sts, k to end.

FRONT

Next row (WS) P4, cast on 7 sts, p4—15 sts. Work in St st until same length as back to rib.

Next row K2tog *p1, k1, rep from *, end p1, k2tog. Rib 1 more row. Bind off.

SLEEVES

Cast on 8 sts. Work in k1, p1 rib for 2 rows.

Work in St st, inc 1 st each side on next row, then every 1½" once—12 sts. Work even until piece measures 3" from beg. Bind off.

COLLAR

Cast on 28 sts. Work in k1, p1 rib for 2 rows. Bind off. Fold in half with WS tog and sew back seam.

FINISHING

Place a marker 1" down from shoulders on front and back. Sew sleeves between markers. Sew side and sleeve seams. Sew collar loosely around neck.

Yarn

Laine Colbert Tapestry Wool by DMC (approx. 8.7yds/8m) wool
3 skeins in #7956 teal

Needles

Size 3 (3mm) needles or size needed to obtain gauge

note

Back and front are worked in one piece from back to front with an opening for the neck.

gauge

5 sts and 8 rows to 1" over St st using size 3 (3mm) needles. FOR PROPER FIT, TAKE THE TIME TO CHECK YOUR GAUGE.

Diamond Dress

Diamond decadence. Diamonds are a doll's best friend, and this many–carated classic is no exception. Its smart sheath shape and bold diamond design lend sparkle to a springtime outing. The wide off–the–shoulder foldover collar gives the crowning touch. The dress is knit in one flat piece in stockinette with intarsia diamonds and ribbed collar, then sewn up with one back seam.

Yarn
Retors a Broder by DMC
(11yd/10m) 4 skeins of #2563
green (A)
Retors Mat by DMC
(11yd/10m) 1 skein of white
(B)
Needles
Size 1 (2.25mm) needles or
size to obtain gauge.
Accessories
1 small snap

Dress

With A cast on 39 sts. K 1 row,
p 1 row. K next row on WS for
turning ridge.
P 1 row.

Beg Chart

K16, work 7 sts of diamond chart,
work to end. Cont as established,
working 6-row rep of chart 7 times,
then work rows 1-4.

Armhole Shaping

K9 (right back), bind off 3 sts, join
yarn, k5, work 7 sts diamond chart,
k5, (front) bind off 3 sts, join yarn,
work to end (left back). Cont as
established, casting on 3 sts over
bound off sts on next row, through
row 7 of chart. P 1 row. K 1 row, inc
10 sts evenly spaced—49 sts.

Collar

Work in k1, p1 rib for 1".

Next row (RS) Change to B and
p 1 row.
Cont in rib for ½". Bind off

FINISHING

Sew back seam leaving ¾" opening
below ribbed collar. Fold hem to WS
at turning ridge and sew in place.
Sew snap to opening just below
collar. Fold down collar.

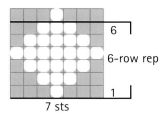

Color Key
▨ Green A
◯ White B

8 sts and 11 rows to 1" over
St st using size 1 (2.25mm)
needles and Retors a Broder.
FOR PROPER FIT, TAKE THE
TIME TO CHECK YOUR GAUGE.

Bold Fair Isle Vest

Well invested.
Stocks may go up and
down, but this fellow's
sense of style never
fluctuates. He's feeling
particularly bullish
today in his bold,
black-and-white Fair
Isle vest, the perfect
business-casual addition
to crisp khakis and an
oxford shirt. The vest is
worked in stockinette
in a classy cotton yarn,
with Fair Isle patterning
duplicate stitched into
its striped design. Tiny
black buttons close
the front.

STRIPE PATTERN

With A, work 4 rows in St st.
Next row *K1 B, k1 A; rep from *,
end k1 B. With B, work 2 rows
in St st.
Next row *P1 A, p1 B; rep from *,
end p1 A.
Work 8 rows in St st with A, 5 rows
with B, 6 rows A, 2 rows B, then
cont with A to end.

vest

BACK

With A, cast on 27 sts. Work in k1,
p1 rib for 2 rows. Work in stripe pat
until piece measures 1¾" from beg.
Armhole Shaping
Bind off 2 sts at beg of next 2 rows,
then bind off 1 st at beg of next 4
rows—19 sts.
Cont in stripe pat until piece
measures 3½" from beg. Bind off.

LEFT FRONT

Cast on 15 sts. Work as for back,
working armhole shaping at beg
of RS rows only, AT SAME TIME,
when piece measures 2½", beg
neck shaping.

Neck Shaping
Dec 1 st at neck edge every other
row 3 times, then every 4th row
twice—6 sts. Work even until same
length as back. Bind off.

RIGHT FRONT
Work to correspond to left front,
reversing all shaping.

FINISHING
Sew shoulder seams.
Armhole Bands
With RS facing and A, pick up and k
27 sts along armhole edge. Work in
k1, p1, rib for 2 rows. Bind off.
Front Band
With RS facing and A, beg at lower
edge of right front, pick up and k 17
sts to first neck dec, 32 sts around
neck to beg of left neck dec, 18 sts
along left front—67 sts. Work in k1
p1 rib for 2 rows. Bind off.
Sew side seams, including armhole
bands. Sew buttons evenly spaced
along left front. Sew on snaps
evenly spaced along front bands.
With B, duplicate st a V in center of
5-row B band on fronts and back.

materials

Yarn
Cotton Perle #3 by DMC, 5g
(approx 10.4yds/15m) cotton
4 skeins in # 823 navy (A)
1 skein in ecru (B)

Needles
Size 1 (2.25mm) needles or
size needed to obtain gauge
Tapestry needle

Accessories
5 JHB #47378 Barbie®
buttons in country blue
3 small snaps

gauge

8 sts and 11 rows to 1" over
St st using size 1 (2.25mm)
needles.
FOR PROPER FIT, TAKE THE
TIME TO CHECK YOUR GAUGE.

Faux Mink Ensemble

Make mine mink. Barbie® is the epitome of elegance in this three-piece ensemble knit in Angora and cashmere. The jacket and hat are worked in garter stitch and stockinette for extra texture. The cashmere skirt decreases in front to a prim point embroidered with a delicate pink-and-sage floral pattern.

PATTERN STITCH
*With B, k 1 row, p 1 row, with A, k 2 rows; rep from * (4 rows) for pat.

jacket

BACK
With larger needles and A, cast on 15 sts. K 2 rows. Work 4-row rep of pat 6 times.
Divide for Fronts
Next row (RS) With B, k6 (right front), join new strand of B, bind off center 3 sts (for neck), work to end (left front). Working both sides at once, with separate strands, work 4-row rep of pat 3 times.
Next row Inc 1 st at front edge every other row twice—8 sts. Cont in pat until fronts measures same length as back. Bind off
Front Band
With RS facing and A, pick up and k 41 sts evenly around front edges. K 1 row. Bind off.

SLEEVES
Place markers 1" down from shoulders on front and back. With larger needles and B, pick up and k 11 sts between markers. Work 4-row rep of pat 6 times. Bind off.

FINISHING
Sew side and sleeve seams. Sew snap to lower edge of fronts.

skirt

With smaller needles and B, cast on 31 sts. Work in k1, p1, rib for 4 rows.
Next row (RS) Knit, inc 16 sts evenly spaced—47 sts. Cont in St st for 2".
Point Decrease
Bind off 2 sts at beg of each row 22 times—3 sts. Bind off. Sew back seam leaving ¾" opening at waist. Sew snap to waist.
Embroidery
With pink, embroider flowers using French knots. Make leaves with green. (Foll photo)

tube top

With smaller needles and B, cast on 39 sts. Work in k1, p1 rib for 2 rows. Work in St st until piece measures 1½" from beg. Work 2 rows in k1, p1 rib. Bind off.
Sew snap to top and bottom. (Close snaps to form tube.)

hat

With smaller needles and A, cast on 22 sts. Work 4 row rep of pat for 3½ times.
Next row K2tog across—11 sts.
Next row P1, *p2tog across; rep from * to end—6 sts. Break yarn and draw through rem sts. Sew back seam.

Yarn
JACKET
Angora by Rainbow Gallery (approx 7yd/6.4m) angora
2 cards in #A21 brown (A)
Cashmere by Rainbow Gallery (approx 9yd/8.2m) cashmere
2 cards in #18 brown (B)
HAT
1 card each in #18 brown (A) and #18 brown (B)
SKIRT
3 cards in #18 brown (B)
TUBE TOP
1 card in #18 brown (B)

Needles
Sizes 2 and 3 (2.5 and 3mm) needles or size needed to obtain gauge

Accessories
1 card each of cashmere #H09 pink and #6 sage for embroidery
4 sets small black snaps

notes

1 Jacket back and front are worked in one piece from the back to the front.
2 Skirt is worked from the waist down.

gauge

8 sts and 12 rows to 1" over St st using 2 (2.5mm) needles and B.
FOR PROPER FIT, TAKE THE TIME TO CHECK YOUR GAUGE.

Polka-Dot Bikini and Coverup

Red hot!
Barbie® is the original beach bunny in this itsy, polka-dot bikini. The halter-style top and trunk-style bottoms are knit in stockinette, then dotted with playful red French knots. A ribbed waistband and a touch of elastic keep the bottoms in place. A red "mesh" cover-up guards against cool ocean breezes; an easy yarn-over pattern creates the lacy look. Both pieces are made of summer-weight cotton.

bikini

BOTTOM
(make 2)
Beg at waist, with 2 strands of A, cast on 20 sts. Work in k1, p1 rib for 2 rows. Work St st for 1¼". Bind off.

POLKA DOTS

With B, embroider a French knot in center of every 4th st across, staggering them every 4th row. With sewing thread, sew front and back seams. Sew center of front to center of back for crotch. Weave elastic thread through rib at waist, pull slightly to gather.

TOP

With 2 strands of A, cast on 40 sts. Work in St st for 1". Bind off. With sewing thread, sew sides tog, gathering the seam for center front. Embroider polka dots as for bottoms.

Straps
(make 2)
With A and crochet hook, ch 4". Fasten off. Sew one strap to each side of top edge, ³⁄₄" from center front.

FINISHING

Lightly block pieces.

lace pattern

(multiple of 2 sts plus 1)
Row 1 (RS) Purl.
Rows 2 and 4 Purl.
Row 3 K1, *yo, ssk; rep from * to end.
Rep rows 1-4 for lace pat.

beach coverup

With 2 strands of yarn held tog, cast on 37 sts.
Row 1 K1, p1, work in lace pat over 33 sts, pl, k1. Cont as established, working 4-row rep of lace pat 9 times and piece measures approx 3" from beg.

Divide for Armholes

Next row (RS) K1, p1, work 7 sts in lace pat, p1, k1 (right front) and place on holder, k2tog, p1, work row 1 of lace pat over next 9 sts, p1, k2tog (back), place rem 11 sts on holder (left front).

BACK

Cont as established, working 4-row rep of lace pat 3 times, then work rows 1-2 once. Bind off 3 sts at beg and end of next row. Place 7 sts on holder for hood.

LEFT FRONT

Attach yarn. K1, p1, work row 1 of lace pat over 7 sts, p1, k1. Cont as established, working 4-row rep of lace pat 3 times, then work rows 1-2 once.
Next row Bind off 3 sts, work to end, place rem 8 sts on holder for hood.

RIGHT FRONT

Attach yarn.
Row 2 (WS) P1, k1, work 7 sts in lace pat, k1, p1. Cont as established, working 4-row rep of lace pat 3 times, then work rows 1-2 once.
Next row K1, p1, work 6 sts in lace pat, bind off last 3 sts, and place rem 8 sts on holder for hood.

HOOD

Place sts from holders onto needle.
Next row (WS) P1, k1, work row 4 of lace pat over next 19 sts, k1, p1— 23 sts. Cont as established, working 4-row rep 6 times. Bind off.
Fold bound-off edge of hood in half and sew tog. Sew shoulder seams.

BIKINI

Yarn
Knit-Cro Sheen by J & P Coats (approx 150yds/135m) cotton 1 ball each in #001 white (A) and #126 red (B)

Needles
Size 2 (2.5mm) needles or size needed to obtain gauge
Size B/1 (2mm) crochet hook

Accessories
Elastic thread
Matching sewing thread

COVERUP

Yarn
Knit-Cro Sheen by J & P Coats (approx 150yds/135m) cotton 1 ball in #126 red

Needles
Size 2 (2.5mm) needles or size needed to obtain gauge
Size B/1 (2mm) crochet hook

Accessories
Stitch holders
Matching sewing thread

notes

1 Work with 2 strands of yarn held tog throughout.
2 Coverup is worked in one piece to the underarm.

gauges

BIKINI
15 sts and 19 rows to 2" over St st using size 2 (2.5mm) needles and 2 strands of yarn held tog.

COVERUP
13 sts and 24 rows to 2" over lace pat using size 2 (2.5mm) needles and 2 strands of yarn held tog.
FOR PROPER FIT, TAKE THE TIME TO CHECK YOUR GAUGES.

Elegant Bride

A day to dream of. Barbie® becomes a fairy-tale bride in a dreamy gown adorned with pearls and silk ribbon. Her billowing skirt features a lace-stitch edging at the hem that changes to an eyelet pattern in the body of the skirt.

STITCH GLOSSARY
SK2P
Sl 1, k2tog, pass sl st over k2tog—2 sts dec.
Double Dec (DD)
Insert RH needle into next 2 sts as if to knit tog and sl to RH needle, k1, pass both sl sts over the knit st—2 sts dec.

lace pattern

(multiple of 10 sts plus 1)
Row 1 (RS) K1, *yo, k3, SK2P, k3, yo, k1; rep from * to end.
Row 2 Purl.
Row 3 P1, *k1, yo, k2, SK2P, k2, yo, k1, p1; rep from * to end.
Rows 4 and 6 *K1, p9; rep from *, end k1.
Row 5 P1, *K2, yo, k1, SK2P, k1, yo, k2, p1; rep from * to end.
Row 7 P1, *K3, yo, SK2P, yo, k3, p1; rep from * to end.
Row 8 Purl.
Row 9 K1, *k3, yo, SK2P, yo, k4; rep from * to end.

Yarn
Cotton Perle by DMC, (approx 48yds/45m) cotton
3 balls in #5 ecru
Needles
Size 1 (2.25mm) needles or size needed to obtain gauge
Accessories
3 size small snaps
½ yard of ecru netting
1 piece of ecru satin lining (optional) 16" wide by 6" long
3mm round pearls in ecru
4 yards of ⅛" wide ecru ribbon
Miniature silk flowers: calla lily or flowers of your choice.

notes

1 Pearls are sewn on after garment is made.
2 Gown is worked in one piece.

gauge

10 sts and 14 rows to 1" over St st using size 1 (2.25mm) needles.
FOR PROPER FIT, TAKE THE TIME TO CHECK YOUR GAUGE.

Elegant Bride

It ends at mid-hip, where stockinette stitch is used to create a long, fitted bodice with dainty pearl buttons down the back and a picot edge at the top. The off-shoulder sleeves, also trimmed with picot, decrease to a point that ends right at the ring finger.

gown

Cast on 131 sts. Work rows 1-9 of lace pat once, then rep rows 8 and 9 until skirt measures 5" from beg.

Next (dec) row (RS) K4 *SK2P, k7; rep from *, end SK2P, k4—105 sts. P 1 row.

Next (dec) row K3 * SK2P, k5; rep from *, end SK2P, k3—79 sts. P 1 row.

Next (dec) row K2 * SK2P, k3; rep from *, end SK2P, k2—53 sts. P 1 row.

Next (dec) row K9, [SK2P, k1] 3 times, k12, [SK2P, k1] 3 times, k8—41 sts.

Work 6 rows in St st.

P10, pm, p21, pm, p10.

Waist Darts

Next (dec) row (RS) K4, DD, k3 (left back), sl marker, k4, DD, k7, DD, k4 , (front), sl marker, k3, DD, k4 (right back)—33 sts. P 1 row.

Next (dec) row K3, DD, k2, sl marker, k3, DD, k5, DD, k3, sl marker, k2, DD, k3—25 sts. Work 6 rows in St st.

BODICE

Next (inc) row (RS) K3, M1, k3 (left back), sl marker, k3, M1, k7, M1, k3 (front) sl marker, k3, M1, k3 (right back)—29 sts. P 1 row.

Next (inc) row K4, M1, k3, sl marker, k4, M1, k7, M1, k4, sl marker, k3, M1, k4—33 sts. P 1 row.

Next (inc) row K5, M1, k3, sl marker, k5, M1, k7, M1, k5, sl marker, k3, M1 k5—37 sts. P 1 row.

Next (inc) row K6, M1, k3, sl marker, k6, M1, k7, M1, k6, sl marker, k3, M1, k6—41 sts. Work in St st for 1".

Picot Edging

Row 1 K1, *yo, k2tog; rep from * to end.

Rows 2 and 4 Purl.

Row 3 and 5 Knit.

Bind off.

FINISHING

Sew back seam, leaving open 2½" from top. Turn picot hem to inside and sew in place.

Back Bands

With RS facing, pick up and k 22 sts along side right edge of back. K 4 rows. Bind off. Rep for left back. Sew snaps to gown evenly spaced along back bands. Sew 9 pearls evenly spaced along right back band. Sew pearls around top of gown on each picot point. Sew pearls to form a V at center. Sew a pearl to each eyelet point around lower edge of skirt (foll photo).

Weave ribbon in and out of skirt along each vertical eyelet and stitch in place at top edge.

Yarn

Cotton Perle by DMC, (approx 48yds/45m) cotton 3 balls in #5 ecru

Needles

Size 1 (2.25mm) needles or size needed to obtain gauge

Accessories

3 size small snaps
½ yard of ecru netting
1 piece of ecru satin lining (optional) 16" wide by 6" long
3mm round pearls in ecru
4 yards of ⅛" wide ecru ribbon
Miniature silk flowers: calla lily or flowers of your choice.

notes

1 Pearls are sewn on after garment is made.
2 Gown is worked in one piece.

gauge

10 sts and 14 rows to 1" over St st using size 1 (2.25mm) needles.

FOR PROPER FIT, TAKE THE TIME TO CHECK YOUR GAUGE.

Elegant Bride

A layered, pearled, full-length veil topped with a Juliet cap adds the crowning touch, and the bouquet, made of calla lilies with a pearl ribbon bow and streamers, is far too pretty to throw.

LINING (OPTIONAL)
Using ½" seam allowance, sew short sides tog. Fold each long side down ½" and sew in place. Gather top of lining to fit skirt and sew to skirt.

SLEEVES
Beg at upper edge and cast on 15 sts. Work 4 rows in St st. Work picot edging as for gown, then cont in St st for 1".
Next (dec) row (RS) K1, ssk, k to last 3 sts, k2tog, k1—13 sts.
Rep dec row every 8th row twice more—9 sts. Work even until piece measures 2½" from picot edge.
Point Shaping
Next row (RS) K1, ssk, k to last 3 sts, k2tog, k1—7 sts. P 1 row.
Rep last 2 rows once more—5 sts.
Next row (RS) K1, SK2P, k1—3 sts.
Sl 1, p2tog, psso. Fasten off.

FINISHING
Turn picot hem to inside and sew in place. Sew sleeve seam. Sew pearls to points on picot edging. Attach sleeve to gown at underarm.

cap
Cast on 37 sts. Work 4 rows in St st. Work picot edge as for gown, then cont in St st for ½".
Next (dec) row (RS) K1, *SK2P across—13 sts. P 1 row.
Rep dec row—5 sts.
Pass last 4 sts over 1st. Fasten off.

FINISHING
Turn picot hem to inside and sew in place. Sew back seam. Sew pearls to picot points.

VEIL
Cut 2 pieces of net 11½" x 24" and 7" x 24". Place shorter piece over longer one and gather long edge of both pieces to 1" and sew to back of cap. Round the corners and sew pearls to lower edge of each piece..

bouquet
Wrap small piece of net around calla lily. Cut a 14" piece of ribbon. Sew 10 pearls to each edge of ribbon spaced evenly apart. Tie into a bow around flowers.

Yarn
Cotton Perle by DMC, (approx 48yds/45m) cotton
3 balls in #5 ecru
Needles
Size 1 (2.25mm) needles or size needed to obtain gauge
Accessories
3 size small snaps
½ yard of ecru netting
1 piece of ecru satin lining (optional) 16" wide by 6" long
3mm round pearls in ecru
4 yards of ⅛" wide ecru ribbon
Miniature silk flowers: calla lily or flowers of your choice.

notes

1 Pearls are sewn on after garment is made.
2 Gown is worked in one piece.

gauge

10 sts and 14 rows to 1" over St st using size 1 (2.25mm) needles.
FOR PROPER FIT, TAKE THE TIME TO CHECK YOUR GAUGE.

Bags For All Occasions

In the bag.
Whether out for an evening on the town, a day at the beach, or a weekend away, Barbie has just the tote for her treasures. A blue wool shoulder bag features a clever cable down the center, while her variegated wool purse goes with nearly everything and clasps shut with a crystal bead.

cable bag

3-ST RC
K the 3rd st on LH needle, k the first st, then k the 2nd st and sl all 3 sts from LH needle tog.

bag

Cast on 17 sts. K 1 row.
Beg Cable Pat
Rows 1 and 3 (WS) P2, k2, p1, k2, p3, k2, p1, k2, p2.
Row 2 (RS) K2, p2, sl 1, p2, k3, p2, sl 1, p2, k2.
Row 4 K2, p2, sl 1, p2, 3-st RC, p2, sl 1, p2, k2.
Cont to work cable pat, working 4-row rep 8 times more. Bind off.

STRAP
Cast on 50 sts. Bind off.

FINISHING
Fold bag in half with WS tog. Sew side seams. Sew strap to each side of bag. Sew snap to WS of center front.

variegated bag

BACK

Cast on 8 sts. K 2 rows. Cont in garter st, inc 1 st each side on next row, then every other row 2 times more—14 sts. Work even until piece measures 1¾" from beg, end with a WS row.

Flap

Next (dec) row (RS) Ssk, k to last 2 sts, k2tog. K 1 row. Rep last 2 rows twice more—8 sts. Bind off.

FRONT

Cast on 8 sts. K 2 rows. Cont in garter st, inc 1 st each side on next row, then every other row 2 times more—14 sts. Work even until piece measures 1¾" from beg. End with WS row. Bind off.

HANDLE

Cast on 30 sts. K 1 row. Bind off.

FINISHING

Sew front to back. Sew strap to each side. Fold flap down. Sew bead to outside of flap.

materials

CABLE BAG

Yarn

Paternayan Persian by JCA (approx 8yd/7.4m) wool
2 skeins in #555 pale blue

Accessories

1 snap

VARIEGATED BAG

Yarn

Painter's Palette Premium Merino by Koigu Wool Design, 1¾oz/50g (approx 175yds/161m) wool
Small amount in variegated blue

Accessories

One matching bead

NEEDLES FOR ALL BAGS

Size 1 (2.25mm) needles or size needed to obtain gauge

note

CABLE BAG

Use 2 plys of yarn held tog throughout.

gauges

CABLE BAG

8 sts and 10 rows to 1" over cable pat using size 1 (2.25mm) needles and 2 plys of Paternayan Persian Yarn held tog.

VARIEGATED BAG

7 sts and 18 rows to 1" over garter st using size 1 (2.25mm) needles and Painter's Palette Premium Merino.
FOR PROPER SIZE, TAKE THE TIME TO CHECK YOUR GAUGES.

Bags For All Occasions

The pink patchwork bag is worked in intarsia blocks—and it's just the size for a carrying a knitting project—but only sunshine and happiness fit in the sunflower shoulder bag, made with two knitted flowers.

flower bag

FLOWER

(make 2)

With A, cast on 55 sts. K 2 rows.

Rows 1, 3 and 5 (WS) With A, purl.

Rows 2 and 4 (RS) With A, k1, *yo, k2, ssk, k2tog, k2, yo, k1; rep from * to end.

Row 6 With A, k1, k2tog, *ssk, [k2tog] twice, k1, k2tog; rep from *, end ssk, [k2tog] twice, k1—31 sts.

Rows 7 and 9 With B, purl.

Row 8 With B, k1, *k2tog, ssk; rep from *, end k2tog—16 sts.

Row 10 With B, k1 *k2tog; rep from *, end k1—9 sts.

Row 11 With B, [p2tog] 4 times, p1—5 sts.

Pass last 4 sts over first st. Fasten off.

STRAP

With C, cast on 55 sts. Bind off.

FINISHING

Block flower lightly. With A, using short straight sts, embroider seeds on black center. Sew WS tog leaving 1" open at top. Sew on strap.

PATCHWORK BAG
Yarn
Cotton Perle by DMC, (approx 16.4yds/15m) cotton
1 skein each in #601 fuchsia (A), #605 light pink (B), #3685 berry (C), and #316 mauve (D)

Needles
Size 1 (2.25mm) needles or size needed to obtain gauge

FLOWER BAG
Yarn
Cotton Perle by DMC, (approx 16.4 yds/15m) cotton
1 skein each in #444 yellow (A), # 310 black (B), and #368j green (C)

Needles
Size 1 (2.25mm) needles or size needed to obtain gauge

patchwork bag

NOTE
With A, cast on 22 sts.
*Next row (RS) K6 A, k5 B, k5 C, k6 D.
Cont as established for 5 rows more.
Next row (RS) K6 B, k5 C, k5 D, k6 A.
Cont as established for 5 rows more.
Next row (RS) K6 C, k5 D, k5 A, k6 B.
Cont as established for 5 rows more.
Next row (RS) K6 D, k5 A, k5 B, k6 C.
Cont as established for 5 rows more.
Rep from * once more—48 rows.
With A, k 1 row. Bind off with A.

STRAPS
(make 2)
With A cast on 22 sts. Bind off 22 sts.

FINISHING
Fold bag in half with WS tog. Sew side seams. Sew one strap to front and one strap to back, centering on blocks.

note

PATCHWORK BAG
When changing colors, twist yarns on WS to prevent holes.

gauge

PATCHWORK AND FLOWER BAGS

8 sts and 10 rows to 1" over St st using size 1 (2.25mm) needles and Cotton Perle. FOR PROPER SIZE, TAKE THE TIME TO CHECK YOUR GAUGE.

Bags For All Occasions

The chic cashmere handbag, embroidered with tiny flowers, should be in every woman's closet. Even Ken® will want to borrow the unisex satchel, knit in a velvety yarn that looks just like suede.

cashmere bag

With MC, cast on 22 sts. Work in St st until piece measures 3½".
Flap
Next (dec) row K1, ssk, k to last 3 sts, k2tog, k1. P 1 row.
Rep last 2 rows once more—18 sts.
Next row K1, ssk, slip k1 over ssk, bind off center 12 sts, k2tog and pass last bound-off st over k2tog, bind off last st.

FINISHING
Work floral embroidery on front foll photo—work 4 lazy daisy flowers in pink, stem stitch stems and lazy daisy leaves in green. Sew beads to flower centers. Make a 4" twisted cord for strap. With WS tog, fold piece in half, leaving ½" at top for flap. Sew side seams. Sew strap to each side. Sew snap to center of flap and front.

dress by Mattel©

CASHMERE BAG
Yarn
Cashmere by Rainbow Gallery
(approx 9yds/8.2m) cashmere
2 cards in #H12 lavender (MC)
1 card each in #HO9 pink and
#HO6 green (for embroidery)
Needles
Size 0 (2mm) needles or size
needed to obtain gauge
Accessories
4 small seed beads in
corresponding colors
One small snap
SUEDE SATCHEL
Yarn
Very Velvet by Rainbow Gallery
(approx 10yds/9.1m) nylon
1 card in #U258 brown
Accessories
Small black seed bead
Needles
Size 1 (2.25mm) needles or
size needed to obtain gauge

suede satchel

Cast on 15 sts. Work in St st
for 1½". K next row on WS for
turning ridge.
Cont in St st until piece measures
1½" from turning ridge. K next row
on WS for turning ridge.
Next (dec) row (RS) K1, ssk, k to
last 3 sts, k2tog, k1. P 1 row. Rep
last 2 rows 4 times—5 sts. Then rep
dec row once more—3 sts.
Next row (WS) P1, p2tog, pass the
p1 over the p2tog. Fasten off.

HANDLE
Cast on 12 sts. Bind off.

FINISHING
With WS tog, fold piece at first
turning ridge and sew side seams.
Sew handle to center top. Fold flap
down at turning ridge. Sew bead to
point of flap.

gauge

CASHMERE BAG
9 sts and 12 rows to 1" over
St st using size 0 (2mm)
needles and Cashmere.
SUEDE SATCHEL
8 sts and 12 rows to 1" over
St st using size 1 (2.25mm)
needles and Velvet.
FOR PROPER SIZE, TAKE THE
TIME TO CHECK YOUR GAUGE.

Evening Glamour Ensemble

Stepping out. Barbie® is ready for an evening at the opera in this majestic ensemble. Her glorious full-length skirt shimmers in gold and black metallic yarn. A feathery black shell, knit in a fluffy novelty yarn, adds a strain of sweet harmony, and her tiny gold evening bag is the perfect size for opera glasses and a handkerchief.

skirt

With smaller needles and A, cast on 75 sts. Work in St st for 4 rows.
Next (picot) row (RS) K1, *yo, k2tog; rep from * to end.
P 1 row, k 1 row, p 1 row.
Next row (RS) Change to B and k 1 row, p 1 row. Change to A and k 1 row, p 1 row.
Rep last 4 rows (for stripe pat) 15 times more. Piece measures approx 6".
Next (dec) row (RS) Change to B. K2tog across, end k1—38 sts.
P 1 row.
Next (dec) row (RS) Change to A. K1, k2tog across, end k1—20 sts.
P 1 row.
Next (dec) row (RS) Change to B. Knit, cast on 4 sts at end of row—24 sts. Work in k1, p1 rib for 3 rows. Bind off in rib.

FINISHING
Turn hem to WS at picot row and sew in place. Sew back seam leaving 1" open at waist. Sew snap to waist.

top

With larger needle and Artic Rays, cast on 18 sts. Work in garter st for 1".
Armhole Shaping
Next row (RS) K10, bind off 4 sts, k4. Cast on 4 sts over bound-off sts on next row.
Work even in garter st for 2". Rep armhole dec. Work even in garter st for 1" more. Bind off.

FINISHING
Sew 3 snaps evenly spaced along back.

bag

With A, cast on 11 sts. Work in St st for 2".
Flap
Next (dec) row K1, ssk, k to last 3 sts, k2tog, k1. P 1 row.
Rep last 2 rows twice more—5 sts.
Next row K1, SK2P, k1—3 sts.
Next row P1, p2tog, psso.
Fasten off.

FINISHING
With WS tog, fold up lower edge to flap and sew side seams. Sew 3 seed beads to flap point. Fold down flap.

Yarn
Cresta d'Oro by Rainbow Gallery (approx 15yds/ 13m) viscose
2 cards each in CO4 gold (A) and C10 black (B)
Artic Rays Wispy Fringe by Rainbow Gallery (approx 8yds/7.3m) nylon
2 cards in #Ar1 black
Needles
Sizes 1 and 2 (2.25 and 2.5mm) needles or size needed to obtain gauge
Accessories
4 small black snaps
BAG
Yarn
Cresta d'Oro by Rainbow Gallery (approx 15yds/ 13m) viscose
1 card in CO4 gold
Needles
Size 1 (2.25mm) needles or size needed to obtain gauge
Accessories
3 small seed beads in gold

note

Top is worked sideways in one piece.

gauges

SKIRT AND BAG
7 sts and 11 rows to 1" over St st using size 1 (2.25mm) needles and Cresta d'Oro.
TOP
7 sts and 10 rows to 1" over St st using size 2 (2.5mm) needles and Artic Rays.
FOR PROPER FIT, TAKE THE TIME TO CHECK YOUR GAUGES.

Beachwear Bonanza

Sun-kissed.
It's a hot time in the tropics, but these sun-lovers are well-suited to the occasion in bright beachwear. An elastic yarn in cool Caribbean colors makes the scantiest of suits stay put. All are knit in stockinette and edged with contrasting garter-stitch trim.

two-piece top

With B, cast on 45 sts. K 4 rows.
Change to A and work in St st for 2
rows.
Next row (RS) K18, pm, M1, k9, M1,
pm, k18—47 sts.
P 1 row.
Next row (RS) K18, sl marker, M1,
k11, M1, sl marker, k18—49 sts.
P 1 row.
Next row (RS) K18, sl marker, M1,
k13, M1, sl marker, k18—51 sts.
P 1 row.
K 1 row, p 1 row.
Change to B and k 4 rows. Bind off.
Sew back seam.

two-piece bottom

With B, cast on 51 sts. K 4 rows.
Change to A and work in St st for 1",
end with a WS row.
Next row (WS) *P2, p2tog; rep
from *, end p3—39 sts. P 1 row.
Change to B and k 3 rows. Bind off.
Sew back seam. Sew front to back at
center of lower edge for crotch seam.

swimsuit

STRIPE PATTERN
*2 rows B, 2 rows A; rep from * (4
rows) for stripe pat.

With A, cast on 51 sts. K 2 rows.
Work in stripe pat until piece
measures 1" from beg.
Next row (RS) *K2, k2tog; rep from *
end k3—39 sts. Work 3 rows even.

Top Shaping
Next (dec) row (RS) K1, ssk, k to
last 3 sts, k2tog, k1. P 1 row.
Rep last 2 rows 7 times more—23 sts.
Then rep dec row every 4th row 5
times—13 sts. Work even until piece
measures 4" from beg, end with 2
rows A. Place sts on holder.
Neckband and Tie
Cast on 12 sts and k across sts from
holder, cast on 12 sts—37 sts. K 2
rows. Bind off.

FINISHING
Sew back seam. Sew center front
of cast-on edge to back for
crotch seam. Sew snap to neckband.

trunks

(make 2)
With B, cast on 37 sts. K 4 rows.
Change to A and work in St st until
piece measures ³/₄" from beg.
Bind off 3 sts at beg of next 2
rows—31 sts.
Next row Dec 1 st each side—29 sts.
Work 1 row even.
Rep last 2 rows twice more—25 sts.
Work even until piece measures 1³/₄"
from beg. Place sts on holder.
Waistband
With B, k across sts from both
holders. Work in St st for 3 rows, dec
16 sts evenly spaced across last WS
row—34 sts. K 3 rows. Bind off.

FINISHING
Sew center back and front seam.
Sew leg seam.

TWO-PIECE
Yarn
Rainbow Elastic #3 by K1C2,
LLC (approx 25yds/22.5m)
elastic
1 card each in #56 pink (A)
and #18 blue (B)
Needles
Size 2 (2.5mm) needles or
size needed to obtain gauge
Accessories
Stitch markers
TRUNKS
Yarn
Rainbow Elastic #3 by K1C2
(approx 25yds/22.5m) elastic
1 ball each in #16 blue (A)
and #11 orange (B)
Needles
Size 2 (2.5mm) needles or
size needed to obtain gauge
Accessories
Stitch holders
SWIMSUIT
Yarn
Rainbow Elastic #3 by K1C2
(approx 25yds/22.5m) elastic
1 card each in #124 green (A)
and #2 white (B)
Needles
Size 2 (2.5mm) needles or
size needed to obtain gauge
Accessories
Stitch holder
One small snap

gauge
9 sts and 16 rows to 1" over
St st using size 2 (2.5mm)
needles and Rainbow
Elastic #3.
FOR PROPER FIT, TAKE THE
TIME TO CHECK YOUR GAUGE.

Rich Red Evening Gown with "Fur" Trim

High society.
This glamorous gown
hits the high notes on
any special occasion.
The sleek sheath
silhouette glimmers
in metallic red, while
fabulously fluffy Angora
trims the boat neck, bell
sleeves, and hem. A
daring back slit finishes
off the sophisticated
look, making it perfect
for a night on the town.

gown

With smaller needles and A, cast on 51 sts. Work in St st for 7¾", end with a WS row.

Next row (RS) K12 (left back), join new yarn and bind off 3 sts, k21 (front), join new yarn and bind off 3 sts, k12 (right back). Working all sections at once, cont in St st until piece measures 8" from beg. Bind off.

SLEEVES

With smaller needles and A, cast on 31 sts. K 1 row, p 1 row.

Next (dec) row K1, ssk, k to last 3 sts, k2tog, k1. P 1 row. Rep last 2 rows 8 times more—13 sts. Work 4 rows in St st. Inc 1 st each side on next row, then every other row twice more—19 sts. Work even in St st until piece measures 3" from beg. Bind off 3 sts at beg of next 2 rows, 1 st at beg of next 2 rows. Bind off rem 11 sts.

FINISHING

Beg at 4¼" from cast-on edge and sew a 3" seam, leaving 1" open at top and 4¼" open at bottom. Sew sleeve seams. Sew sleeves to gown at underarms.

Neck Fur Trim
With larger needles and B, cast on 46 sts. K 1 row, p 1 row. Bind off. With sewing thread, sew around upper edge. Sew snap.

Sleeve Fur Trim
With larger needles and B, cast on 24 sts. K 1 row, p 1 row. Bind off. With sewing thread, sew to sleeve edges.

Lower Fur Trim
With larger needles and B, cast on 46 sts. K 1 row, p 1 row. Bind off. With sewing thread, sew around lower edge.

materials

Yarn
Party by Grignasco/JCA, .88oz/25g (approx 191yds/176m) cupro/polyester
1 ball in #63 red (A)
Angora by Rainbow Gallery (each card approx 7yds/6.4m) angora
2 cards in RA01 white (B)

Needles
Sizes 1 and 2 (2.25 and 2.5mm) needles or size needed to obtain gauge

Accessories
1 snap
Matching sewing thread

note

Back and front are worked in one piece to the underarm.

gauge

10 sts and 12 rows to 1" over St st using size 1 needles and Party.
FOR PROPER FIT, TAKE THE TIME TO CHECK YOUR GAUGE.

Belle Party Dress and Gown

Dancing divas. Barbie® won't be a wallflower in this glittering party dress. Knit in metallic magenta, this little number features a tiered, flounced hem worked in bell stitch that decreases to a fetchingly fitted rib skirt and bodice. The neckline repeats the ruffle, which dips demurely off the shoulders. If desired, the body of the dress can be lengthened for a glamorous evening look.

EDGE PATTERN
(worked over 111 sts, decreased by 39 sts)
Row 1 (RS) P3 *k9, p3; rep from * to end.
Row 2 K3 *p9, k3; rep from * to end.
Row 3 P3, *SKP, k5, k2tog, p3; rep from * to end—93 sts.
Row 4 K3, *p7, k3; rep from * to end.
Row 5 P3, *SKP, k3, k2tog, p3; rep from * to end—75 sts.
Row 6 K3, *p5, k3; rep from * to end.
Row 7 P3, *SKP, k1, k2tog, p3; rep from * to end—57 sts.
Row 8 K3, *p3, k3; rep from * to end.
Row 9 P3, *SK2P, p3; rep from * to end—39 sts.
Row 10 K3, *p1, k3; rep from * to end.
Row 11 P3, *k1, p3; rep from * to end.
Row 12 Rep row 10.

RIB PATTERN
Row 1 (RS) P3, *k1, p3: rep from * to end.
Row 2 K3 *p1, k3; rep from * to end.
Rep rows 1 and 2 for rib pat.

dress

Cast on 111 sts. Work bell edging—39 sts.
Work in rib pat for 4". Bind off.
Sew back seam.
Ruffle
(make 2)
Cast on 111 sts. Work bell edging.
Bind off rem 39 sts.
Sew back seam of ruffle.
Sew 1 ruffle to top of dress leaving ½" open at each side for arms. Sew 2nd ruffle above bell edging.

black fur stole

Cast on 53 sts. Work in garter st for 2". Bind off

DRESS
Yarn
Cresta d'Oro by Rainbow Gallery (approx 15yds/ 137m) viscose
4 cards in #C21 pink
Needles
Size 1 (2.25mm) needles or size needed to obtain gauge
STOLE
Yarn
Angora by Rainbow Gallery (approx 7yds/6.4m) angora
3 cards in #18 black
Needles
Size 3 (3mm) needles or size needed to obtain gauge

gauges

DRESS
9 sts and 10 rows to 1" over rib pat using size 1 (2.25mm) needles and Cresta d'Oro.
STOLE
5 sts and 10 rows to 1" over garter st using size 3 (3mm) needles and Angora.
FOR PROPER FIT, TAKE THE TIME TO CHECK YOUR GAUGES.

Sunday Morning Afghan and Cord Rug

Lazy days.
This cashmere/wool afghan adds a soft, warm touch to Barbie® doll's chic decor. It features a basketweave pattern with a fringed edge and pretty embroidered flowers. Cleverly worked in I-cord and coiled into an oblong shape, the cord rug lends old-fashioned charm. The variegated pastels add to the "rag rug" look.

PATTERN STITCH
Rows 1, 3, 5, 7, 9 K1, p1, k1, p1, k7, *p7, k7; rep from *, end p1, k1, p1, k1.
Rows 2, 4, 6, 8, 10 P1, k1, p1, k1, p7, *k7, p7; rep from *, end k1, p1, k1, p1.
Rows 11, 13, 15, 17, 19 K1, p1, k1, p1, p7, *k7, p7; rep from *, end p1, k1, p1, k1.
Rows 12, 14, 16, 18, 20 P1, k1, p1, k1, k7, *p7, k7; rep from *, end k1, p1, k1, p1.
Rep rows 1-20 for pat st.

afghan

Cast on 57 sts. Work in pat st until piece measures 7", end with row 10. Bind off.

FINISHING
Block piece.
Using a single strand, make fringe ½" long at every other stitch on top and bottom edges.
Using lazy daisy st, embroider flowers, alternating colors diagonally. Add straight st leaves with mint (see photo).

cord rug

Rug is worked by making an I-cord, 5 yards long, then sewn tog into an oval shape.

I-cord
Cast on 3 sts. *K3 sts. Do not turn work. Slide sts to right end of needle. Pull yarn to tighten. Rep from * until I-cord measures 5 yards. **Next row** SK2P. Fasten off.

FINISHING
With WS facing, beg at center, fold down 2" and sew tog. Cont to wrap cord around center, sewing in place until all I-cord is used.

materials

AFGHAN
Yarn
Cashwool by Lang/Berroco, Inc., (approx 167yd/152m) cashmere/wool
1 ball of #0020 blue
Small amount of pink, yellow and mint
Needles
Size 2 (2.5mm) needles or size needed to obtain gauge
RUG
Yarn
Knit Cro-Sheen by J.P. Coats (approx 150yds/135m) cotton
1 ball in multi
Needles
Two size 2 (2.5mm) double pointed needles (dpn)
Accessories
Sewing needle
Coordinating sewing thread

sizes

AFGHAN
Approx 7½" x 8"
(including fringe)
RUG
Approximately 6" x 7" oval

note

RUG
Rug can be made smaller or larger by working a shorter or longer I-cord.

gauge

AFGHAN
8 sts and 11 rows to 1" over pat st using size 2 (2.5mm) needles and Cashwool.
FOR PROPER SIZE, TAKE THE TIME TO CHECK YOUR GAUGE.

Abbreviations

approx approximately

beg begin(ning)

bind off Used to finish an edge and keep stitches from unraveling. Lift the first stitch over the second, the second over the third, etc.

cast on A foundation row of stitches placed on the needle in order to begin knitting.

CC contrast color

ch chain(s)

cont continue(ing)

dec decrease(ing)–Reduce the stitches in a row (knit 2 together).

dpn double-pointed needle(s)

foll follow(s)(ing)

g gram(s)

garter stitch Knit every row. Circular knitting: knit one round, then purl one round.

inc increase(ing)–Add stitches in a row (knit into the front and back of a stitch).

k knit

k2tog knit 2 stitches together

LH left-hand

lp(s) loop(s)

m meter(s)

M1 make one stitch–With the needle tip, lift the strand between last stitch worked and next stitch on the left-hand needle and knit into the back of it. One knit stitch has been added.

M1-p make one purl stitch–With the needle tip, lift the strand between last stitch worked and next stitch on the left-hand needle and purl into the back of it. One purl stitch has been added.

MC main color

mm millimeter(s)

oz ounce(s)

p purl

p2tog purl 2 stitches together

pat(s) pattern

pick up and knit (purl) Knit (or purl) into the loops along an edge.

pm place markers–Place or attach a loop of contrast yarn or purchased stitch marker as indicated.

psso pass slip stitch(es) over

rem remain(s)(ing)

rep repeat

rev St st reverse Stockinette stitch–Purl right-side rows, knit wrong-side rows. Circular knitting: purl all rounds.

rnd(s) round(s)

RH right-hand

RS right side(s)

sc single crochet

sk skip

SKP Slip 1, knit 1, pass slip stitch over knit 1.

SK2P Slip 1, knit 2 together, pass slip stitch over the knit 2 together.

sl slip–An unworked stitch made by passing a stitch from the left-hand to the right-hand needle as if to purl.

sl st slip stitch

ssk slip, slip, knit–Slip next 2 stitches knitwise, one at a time, to right-hand needle. Insert tip of left-hand needle into fronts of these stitches from left to right. Knit them together. One stitch has been decreased.

sssk Slip next 3 sts knitwise, one at a time, to right-hand needle. Insert tip of left-hand needle into fronts of these stitches from left to right. Knit them together. Two stitches have been decreased.

st(s) stitch(es)

St st Stockinette stitch–Knit right-side rows, purl wrong-side rows. Circular knitting: knit all rounds.

tbl through back of loop

tog together

WS wrong side(s)

wyib with yarn in back

wyif with yarn in front

work even Continue in pattern without increasing or decreasing.

yd yard(s)

yo yarn over–Make a new stitch by wrapping the yarn over the right-hand needle.

* = repeat directions following * as many times as indicated.

[ ] = Repeat directions inside brackets as many times as indicated.

Helpful Hints

Included here is a basic schematic for a handknit sweater for your Barbie doll. My suggested needle sizes are 000, 00, 0, 1, 2 and 3, the corresponding yarns that work best are crochet cottons, and fingering- and sport-weight yarns. Larger needles and heavier yarns can look big and unflattering on your doll. I've used a wide range of fine yarns including cottons, silks, mohairs, novelty blends, wool, acrylics, angora, and even cashmere. Knitting for Barbie is a great way to use up leftover yarns. If you don't use the yarns suggested, be sure to get the same gauge given on each piece.

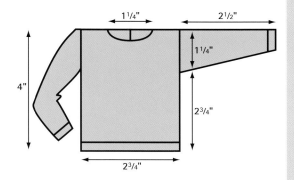

RESOURCES

Berroco, Inc.
PO Box 367
Uxbridge, MA 01569

Coats & Clark
Attn: Consumer Service
PO Box 12229
Greenville, SC 29612-0229

DMC Corporation
Port Kearny bldg. 10A
South Kearny, NJ 07032-4688

Grignasco
Distributed by
JCA, Inc.

JCA, Inc.
35 Scales Lane
Townsend, MA 01469-1094

K1 C2, LLC
2220 Eastman Ave. #105
Ventura, CA 93003

Koigu Wool Designs
R. R. #1
Williamsford, ON N0H 2V0

J & P Coats
Distributed by
Coats & Clark

Lang
Distributed by
Berroco, Inc.

Lion Brand Yarn Co.
34 West 15th Street
New York, NY 10011

Rainbow Gallery
7412 Fulton Ave.
N. Hollywood, CA 91605

Rowan Yarns
5 Northern Blvd.
Amherst, NH 03031

Twice as Nice Design, LTD.
2240 SE 72nd Street
Runnells, IA 50237

JHB Buttons
(800) 525-9007

C. M. Offray & Son, Inc.
Chester, NJ 07930-0601
(908) 879 4700

Acknowledgements

I would like to thank the staff of SoHo Publishing, including Trisha Malcolm, Carla Scott, Chi Ling Moy, Charlotte Parry, Karen Greenwald, Lisa Ventry, Christina Batch and Veronica Manno for doing their jobs so well. Thanks to the photographers for the fun we had shooting these wonderful dolls, and Joe and John Pearl for their transporting. I am grateful to Heris Stenzel, who's professionalism was invaluable to me.

I would also like to acknowledge the magazine editors who have published my Barbie designs in the past, including Pat Harste, Anne Marie Lawson, and Margery Winter.

Special thanks to Anne Brenner, Emily Brenner, Betty Shaver, Diana Book, Anna Masiello, Jenni Stone, Vincent Caputo and Samantha Dornfeld for their encouragement and friendship.

As always, I am forever indebted to Howard Epstein, this time for the many hours he spent with me in toy stores shopping for dolls and accessories.

Thank you to Mattel for allowing me to fulfill the dream of creating this book.

Most of all, I would like to thank Barbara Millicent Roberts from Willows, Wisconsin, for the fun we've shared for so many years.